Copyright Notice & Disclaimer Notice
(Please Read This Before Using This eBook)

The purpose of this ebook is to help people use Next Generation Home Automation (HA 2.0) solutions to make their home more Secure, Safer, Energy Efficient and Enjoyable!

The ability to automate homes has long been the preserve of the more affluent in society. This is no longer the case and Home Automation is now accessible to everyone.

This ebook helps you to understand the amazing lifestyle-enhancing benefits of integrating light control, IP cameras, HA 2.0 alarm systems, multi-room music 2.0 equipment, automated blinds, and smart thermostats into your home!

Mobile devices such as the iPad and smartphones are now the main interface used by adopters of HA 2.0 systems to control all of these systems, and this guide provides you with a step-by-step approach to achieve this functionality at a reasonable cost for your own home!

Published by Gerard O'Driscoll

CONTENTS

DEDICATION

Apparently behind every important guy is a great girl☺This book is dedicated to that girl - my loving wife and girlfriend for over 20 years – Olive! Of course my dedication extends to our five precious children; Aoife (our little GAA star ☺), Ciara (Our little fashion queen), Gerard (AKA Gerdie the hard man), Dearbhla (Our 3 year olde little princess) and latest arrival Baby Aoibhinn (our little thumbelina)☺.

Also a big dedication goes to my Mother and Father living in Dear Olde Skibbereen, West Cork; and my two young brothers – Owen and Brian.

ABOUT THE
AUTHOR

Gerard is 42 years old and originally from Cork in Ireland. Married to Olive with five kids ranging from 1 to 12 years old – so a busy house!

Over the past 20 years, I have served in a variety of management, engineering, and commercial positions in both public and private industry sectors.

I am an accomplished international telecoms expert, educator, serial Internet entrepreneur, angel investor, and home automation integrator. My other professional achievements include the authoring of various technology books:

- IPTV Services and Technologies, Wiley, ISBN: 978-0-470-16372-6 (Published 2008)

- Co-authored Home Technology Integrator Certification Lab: ISBN 1-58122-070-7 Published 2004)

- Essential Guide to Home Networking; ISBN-10: 0130198463 Published (2001)

- Essential Guide to Digital Set-top Boxes and Interactive TV, Prentice Hall,

  ISBN-10: 0130173606 (Published 1999)

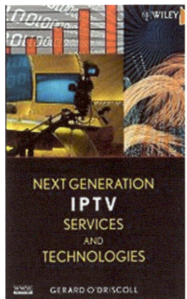 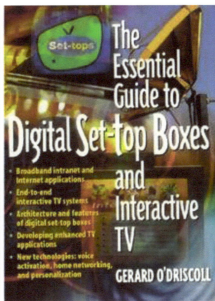 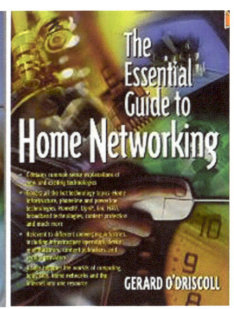

Over the years I have been given the role as commentator on industry events and trends in the digital home industry sector and have been quoted in a number of premier business publications. Additionally I have presented papers at a number of conferences around the world.

In recent times, I have become involved as an angel investor in a portfolio of start-ups & emerging growth companies in mobile apps, e-commerce, e-Learning subscription commerce, food, and digital home sectors.

On the education front, I hold electronics and information technology qualifications from the University of Limerick in Ireland.

Please feel free to subscribe to my blog and get weekly and monthly updates of HA 2.0 developments

If you enjoy this ebook please enter your email to get regular updates from Gerard's blog - HomeAutomation2.0

First Name

Email

Subscribe

Organizational and Topical Coverage

Chapter One: defines HA 2.0, and lists some reasons why you should at least consider installing automation elements of a system, and provides an overview of the various home controller types. The chapter concludes with a categorization of HA 2.0 functionalities, namely essential and nice to have.

Chapter Two: Here I focus on the four most popular technology platforms used by HA 2.0 systems, namely structured wiring, Z-Wave, Insteon, and Zigbee.

Chapter Three: I address readers who wish to gain an in-depth understanding of HA 2.0 alarm systems. In addition to covering the integration of alarm and fire detection systems with your smartphone App, this chapter also deals with adding IP camera, water and freeze alert capabilities to your HA 2.0 system.

Chapter Four: Describes the various benefits of automating your lights at home. Furthermore, the chapter outlines the steps required to install wired and wireless HA 2.0 lighting control systems.

Chapter Five: HA 2.0 systems help you save money by reducing your energy consumption. In this chapter I explain how to use energy saving devices such as smart thermostats to reduce your monthly electricity bill. This chapter also explains how to use your HA 2.0 system to track where and when electricity is used around the house.

Chapter Six: Addresses readers who wish to gain an in-depth understanding of next generation Multi-room Music (MRM) 2.0 systems – both wired and wireless versions! The connection of outdoor weatherproof speakers to your HA 2.0 system is also covered towards the end of this chapter.

Chapter Seven: I explain how to build a multi-zone HDTV distribution system around your house using Cat5e, wireless or Powerline technologies.

Chapter Eight: Describes how to set up an area in your home to support a home cinema. In addition to explaining each of the elements required to build your home cinema system, this chapter also describes how to plan and install a Wi-Fi to IR system – such an addition allows you use a smartphone or tablet to control your home cinema devices in addition to your HA 2.0 system.

Who Should Read This Book

This ebook is intended to be read by the following people:

- Home owners interested in controlling their lighting, alarm, heating and entertainment systems on their smartphones or tablets while out and about or at home.

- Home builders interested in identifying specific home automation ideas that will differentiate their offerings and improve overall property sales.

- This eBook is a useful tool for electrical contractors and alarm installers who are unsure about how to start offering HA 2.0 installation services to their customers.

- Anyone else curious about how to setup a HA 2.0 system at a reasonable cost!

CHAPTER 1

INTRODUCTION TO HOME AUTOMATION 2.0

Home Automation Overview

The first iteration of automation for the residential sector, also known as Home Automation 1.0 (HA 1.0) has been available for the past three decades – primarily confined to high-end households and ambitious technology enthusiasts.

Figure 1.1, illustrates the timeline of the HA 1.0 era:

❏ Figure 1.1 HA 1.0 Timeline

The key features of the above diagram are:

- Mid Seventies – A home automation protocol called X10 was introduced to the marketplace.

- Mid Eighties – New standards were released and failed to gain traction amongst the general population.

- Nineties & early noughties – Although interest in home automation was growing at the end of the 1990s, uptake was dominated by professionally installed proprietary solutions and DIY products based on the X-10 automation protocol.

- Mid noughties to late noughties – X10 products start to lose popularity with the release of next generation standardized products based on – Zigbee, Wifi and Z-Wave.

The failure of HA 1.0 to capture people's imagination has been attributed to a number of reasons, namely:

- **Complexity –** Many of the HA 1.0 products released in the early years of home automation were buggy and technically complex.

- **Multiple incompatible standards –** Over the years there have been attempts by various organizations to create standards to drive the adoption of home automation systems across the globe. Poor interoperability of devices from different suppliers and limited support from the manufacturing community has kept penetration of HA 1.0 products to a minimum.

- **Expensive to install –** Although HA 1.0 did provide for DIY type products, in general an end-to-end home automation system required expensive install professionals to ensure that the equipment worked correctly. Incorporating a full home automation system into a new house required a significant upfront investment.

- **The media –** Coverage of home automation 1.0 systems was typically confined to case studies of large high-end houses owned by celebrities, or demonstrations of futuristic smart homes. This approach has embellished the belief in most people's minds that home automation is not affordable and is only available to affluent people in our society.

- **A solution looking for a problem –** HA 1.0 solutions were nice to have; but did not solve any specific problem for consumers around the globe.

- **Limited to DIY enthusiasts and high-end properties –** The HA 1.0 market is quite small and limited to people who install automation in their homes as a hobby, and to systems that get installed by professional home integration experts.

Today, user perceptions towards home automation have begun to change. People are starting to learn about the possibilities of using their smartphones to control their homes.

What is HA 2.0?

> **"** *No longer is home automation confined to the privileged in society!* **"**

The latest generation of automation, dubbed home automation 2.0 (HA 2.0) is changing the way the average person thinks about controlling their home.

HA 2.0 refers to the ability to use a device such as a standard remote control, a smartphone, tablet, or PC to control particular life enhancement systems within your home. Examples of critical systems you might want to control from anywhere in the world include lighting, heating, alarm, and cameras.

The term often means different things to different people; some people think of HA 2.0 as a system that allows them to turn their heating and lights on from their iPhone whilst on the way home from work, whereas others define an HA 2.0 system as a means of cutting down on energy costs.

What it means in reality is that home automation solutions have reached a stage in their evolution, where it has finally become affordable for the 'man on the street' – no longer is home automation confined to the privileged in society!

HA 2.0 Ecosystem

Almost daily, we hear of new and innovative home automation products being launched onto the marketplace from a diverse range of stakeholders.

Figure 1.2 illustrates the key players within the HA 2.0 ecosystem:

- Manufacturers
- Utility companies
- Telecommunication providers
- Online e-commerce stores
- App developers

● DIY'ers

● System integrators & installers

❏ **Figure 1.2 – HA 2.0 Industry Ecosystem**

As you can see from the above diagram HA 2.0 is on the way; however, in order for HA 2.0 to achieve mass market uptake, closer cooperation between all of these stakeholders will be required over the coming years.

HA 2.0 Market Drivers

Home Automation is positioned at the nexus of the following eight booming market trends:

Standardization has happened! – Global standards, protocols, and data distribution systems are available, which allow home automation control structures such as security and lighting systems to interact and integrate with each other.

The Internet – The wide adoption of the Internet has resulted in the growth and advancement of HA 2.0. Users can activate an App running on their smartphone or tablet device to remotely access their surveillance cameras, adjust home lights, turn up the air conditioning or close their curtains from anywhere in the world.

③ Proliferation of mobile devices such as smartphones and tablets: The near-ubiquitous ownership of smartphones is driving demand for Apps that allow consumers to monitor and control their alarm, lighting, heating, cameras and entertainment systems remotely over the Internet. Awareness that these devices can be used to control all of these in-home systems is starting to slowly creep into society.

④ Availability of Affordable HA 2.0 products: Most HA 2.0 products do not require professional installation and are pretty affordable to buy. Low cost products based on mature technologies such as Z-Wave, Zigbee, INSTEON and Wi-Fi have eliminated the pre-requisite of re-wiring a house to install an automation system.

⑤ Much more than the cool factor: Not only is App control of a person's home considered to be cool, but HA 2.0 products can help to enhance living standards, increase home security levels and cut down on energy expenses.

⑥ Major service providers are reselling HA 2.0 home monitoring products to their customers – Cable operators, telecom companies, large international home security companies are looking for new growth opportunities and have started to offer home control and alarm subscription products to their existing basw of customers.

⑦ Government Initiatives – Governments around the world, including our own here in Ireland, are encouraging the adoption of smart grid technologies in order to reduce household energy consumption. HA 2.0 products such as appliance control modules, automated light switches, and smart thermostats are viewed by most as valued additions to these initiatives.

⑧ Expectations are growing! – People's expectations are growing from generation to generation. In addition to basic telephone and TV services enjoyed by our parents, younger people nowadays (such as myself ☺) want features such as HDTV, multi-room music, surround sound and IP cameras included in their homes.

HA 2.0 Benefits

As with everything in life, the benefits of motivating yourself and spending money needs to produce some tangible results! Although the benefits of adding automation to your home will vary from person to person, there are some general ones that most people can enjoy as result of adding HA 2.0 system to their property:

It's simple to use: Once installed, a HA 2.0 system provides easy control of all your lights, heating, security and entertainment systems via a tablet, smartphone or PC.

Improved comfort & convenience: HA 2.0 systems allow you to setup 'scenes' that will increase comfort levels at home. Scenes are normally used to perform a number of actions at a particular instance in time. For instance, I have an 'ALL OFF' scene on my iPhone that switches all of the lights OFF around the house – it's handier than jumping out of a warm bed on a cold Irish winter's night and turning off the light in the bathroom, which was left on by one of our kids ☺ Popular scenes that you may want to consider once your HA 2.0 system is installed include:

- A scene called 'Heading to Bed', which turns OFF all your lights, arms your alarm in night time mode, turns OFF your music and reduces the set-point levels of your thermostats.

- A scene called 'Wakeup', which turns the music ON at a low level in the bedrooms and main bathroom. Additionally, this scene could also be configured to turn ON the lights at a particular dim level and raise the thermostat set-point levels for the downstairs zone.

- A scene called 'Party', which turns the music ON in all your downstairs rooms, switches ON all of the outside lights and dim lights in your dining area. In winter time, you might also want to consider setting your thermostat to activate the boiler to increase temperature levels around the house.

Enhanced security & safety levels: A HA 2.0 system has the potential to make your family safer. Here are my top three favorite HA 2.0 safety options:

- Receive an instant alert via text message or email that your house is under attack from intruders.

- Receive live video feeds from an IP camera(s) located inside or outside the house to your smartphone.

- When the smoke detector is activated then selected lights around the house will automatically turn on.

Save money: I knew this one would grab your attention L. There is a perception out there that 'fancy' automation systems cost a fortune, where in reality these systems are very affordable and can in fact save you some money. Once installed and configured a HA 2.0 system helps you to save on your monthly electricity, gas, and water bills. In addition to saving money, the implementation of a HA 2.0 system also indirectly contributes a little to improving the environment.

 Increase house value: An easy and engaging way to add value to your home and increase its resale appeal is to upgrade with a HA 2.0 system. Reduced energy costs and high security levels appeal to tech savvy professional house buyers. The addition of a HA 2.0 system to a property helps to make your home stand out from other 'for sale' houses in the area.

 It's fun and provides the Wow factor: There is some really cool stuff you can do with a HA 2.0 system. Not only will you enjoy messing around with it yourself but it also creates the wow effect for neighbors and friends.

 Applies to all home sizes: A HA 2.0 system can be used in all household types ranging from a single bedroom apartment, up to a 2,000 square foot detached house and larger if you're rich ☺

 The Peace of Mind Feeling: Have you ever left the house in a hurry and had this uneasy feeling that you forgot to turn off the lights or indeed lock the door after you – not a nice feeling and puts an element of doubt in your mind. HA 2.0 solves this problem by allowing you to use your smartphone to check the status of the door lock and lights around the house, without having to drive all the way back home.

Types of HA 2.0 Solutions Available

The type of HA 2.0 system that you decide on installing, will depend on whether you are building a new home, or as is the case with most of us, retrofitting your existing home.

 New build HA 2.0 systems – When thinking about putting in home automation products for a new build, then consideration needs to be given to installing a wired based system. Wired based automation systems have a proven track record over the past decade and continue to evolve in line with developments in the world of technology. Experienced installers are typically required to plan, install, program and support your system

Retrofit HA 2.0 systems – Retrofit HA 2.0 systems have mass market appeal and can be self-installed or alternatively (if you live in certain parts of the USA) purchased as part of a monthly service package through a telecommunications or utility company. In most cases, retrofit HA 2.0 systems utilize wireless and Powerline technologies.

HA 2.0 Applications

There are a myriad of applications supported by HA 2.0 systems, ranging from being able to switch off lamps around the house with a smartphone, to automatically executing sophisticated music, heating, security and lighting control tasks.

The types of applications supported by some of the systems available in the market are explained in Table 1.1.

Table 1.1 – HA 2.0 Applications

HA 2.0 Feature	Description
24/7 Burglary & Theft Monitoring	Provide the ability to self-monitor your home via a smartphone or for an additional fee use a monitoring centre to keep an eye on your property 24/7.
Fire & Smoke Monitoring	As the name suggests, smoke and heat detectors help notify at the early stages of a fire risk.
Carbon Monoxide (CO) Monitoring	Sensors notify you if levels of toxic CO gas start to reach dangerous levels.
Monitoring Flood and Water Levels	Once installed, a flood detector notifies you of rising water as it occurs. Such notifications can allow you to take corrective action in real time.
Remote Arm and Disarm Capabilities	Most HA 2.0 products allow you to arm and disarm your security system with an easy to use iPhone, iPad or Android application.
Email and Text Alerts Notifications	The ability to get notified immediately via e-mail or text when a particular event occurs at your home such as a break-in is one of the key functions of next generation HA systems.
Lighting Control	Use your HA 2.0 system to: Turn lights ON or OFF at pre-determined times. Improve energy consumption through the use of motion detectors. Increase life of bulbs by controlling dimming levels.

HA 2.0 Feature	Description
Blind and Curtain Control	A HA 2.0 system can also be used to manage the amount of natural lighting entering your home, by controlling shades, curtains and roller blinds.
Thermostat and Heating Control	Home automation 2.0 systems save you money! Here are some practical ways of using a HA 2.0 system to cut your energy bill: Configure a scene that turns OFF all lights & electrical devices when you're at work. Use your smartphone App to check in and control your boiler remotely. Create an 'ALL OFF' scene that turns OFF all electrical devices that consume phantom current.
Remote Real-Time Video	This feature helps to increase your peace of mind by allowing you to remotely observe your home through indoor and outdoor cameras. In the event that a break-in occurs, the HA 2.0 system will remotely store video clips on the cloud of the event as it happens.
Monitoring Energy Usage	If acted upon, HA 2.0 systems will help you lower your energy bill by showing where and when electricity is being used.
Home Control Touchscreen	Some of the higher-end HA 2.0 systems come with an interactive touch-screen that provides instant access to your security, heating, entertainment and camera systems, whilst at home or away. Of course many of these proprietary touchscreens from the HA 1.0 era are getting replaced with iPads, Windows RT and Android tablets!
Multi-room music and TV	It is possible to use HA 2.0 controllers to link your multi-room music and TV system with sub-systems such as lights, electric blinds and heating.
Aging in place	People in general have a strong desire to remain independent in their own homes as they get older. HA 2.0 products can be tailored to suit the security, energy savings and entertainment requirements of elderly people and those that live alone.

Manage Your Home With a **Smartphone App !**

How Does a HA 2.0 System Operate?

The first point to make with regards to HA 2.0 is that everything in your house will work perfectly fine without your new automation system. In other words, when you walk over to the wall to switch the light on, pressing the toggle works and the light comes on!

The components of a fully rounded end-to-end HA 2.0 system are presented in the diagram below:

❑ **Figure 1.3 End-to-end-HA 2.0 System**

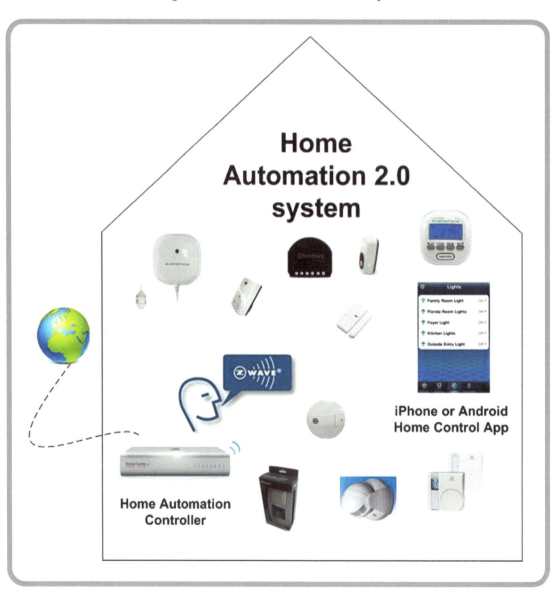

It goes without saying but an Internet service is a pre-requisite for any type of HA 2.0 system. In addition to your broadband service, you will also require a centralized controller unit. This unit in turn communicates with a range of wired and wireless sensors.

The components used to build a HA 2.0 system are often sold in the form of kits. Table 1.2 provides further details on some of the HA monitoring and control kits available on the market.

☐ Table 1.2 – Types of Home Automation Kits

Kit Name	Description
Home Video Monitoring Kit	Typically includes a home automation controller and an IP camera.
Home Alarm Kit	In addition to a home automation controller, security focused kits include door and window sensors, a motion detector and in some cases a key fob.
Home Energy Kits	These kits allow you to manage your home's energy consumption from your smartphone or any Internet enabled device when you are away from home. Smart thermostats, appliance control modules and wireless lighting switches are often included

Kits are available from some telecom providers in the USA and are typically accompanied by a monthly recurring subscription service fee. If you want to avoid the monthly charge then you might want to consider purchasing a self-monitoring kit from an online e-commerce store.

Some type of Mobile App is also provided as part of an end-to-end home automation 2.0 system.

How Much Does a HA 2.0 System Cost?

❝ *The addition of an HA 2.0 system to your home is surprisingly affordable and pretty easy to install.* **❞**

Ensuring that average consumers have access to simple, yet affordable products is one of the main pillars of the HA 2.0 paradigm.

The addition of an HA 2.0 system to your home is surprisingly affordable and pretty easy to install. Many of the newer generation of HA controllers are based on wireless protocols and are pretty easy to set up and get running. There is a perception amongst the general public that home automation systems are very expensive.

Although this perception exists, the current reality is that the price point for introductory HA 2.0 kits here in Europe are between €500 and €1,000, whereas in the USA price points are slightly lower – for instance a $500 kit will provide you with basic smartphone control of your lighting and heating system.

If the automation system is used proactively to manage electricity usage then these types of systems often pay for themselves over a two or three year period.

Now, if you want to really impress the neighbors then installing a multi-room music and HDTV system could set you back a further two to three thousand bucks (Euro for us guys ☺)!

> **! Quick Side Note from ● Gerard:**
> There is typically an additional monthly charge to cover the costs of SMS and video storage services.

As adoption and demand for HA 2.0 systems grow, prices are expected to fall further over the coming years. The real beauty of HA 2.0 systems is that you can start small and grow the system as you can afford it.

How to Build a Smartphone or Tablet Based Home Automation System (6 Steps)

Here are the step-by-step instructions that you need to follow in order to build a system that will allow you to use an iOS, Android or Windows device to control your home.

This section provides a brief overview of each of the steps. Detailed explanations of what you need to do in terms of setting up your own HA 2.0 system are contained in the main chapters.

The process consists of two distinctive parts – as illustrated in Figure 1.4, part one involves implementing three essential home automation functions.

❑ **Figure 1.4 Three Core HA 2.0 System Systems**

Part 1: Essential Home Automation Functions

In my humble opinion there are certain household functions that are absolutely critical to everyone – ensuring that your family is safe, comfortable and secure in your home.

STEP 1
Adding Family Security & Safety Systems to your HA 2.0 Controller

Enhancing the security in your home can be as simple as adding wired or wireless motion detector(s), door, and window contacts. Once a sensor is tripped by your 'Visitor' then a signal is automatically sent to the home automation controller. The controller in turn sends you a text message or email notifying you in real time of the break-in!

Another method of enhancing home or indeed business security is to integrate an IP camera with your home control system. IP cameras are available for inside or outside and come in wired or Wi-Fi versions. The images relayed from these cameras can be viewed from anywhere in the world via an Internet browser. When an IP camera is added to your home network, you will be able to configure your home automation controller to send images onto a cloud server once an intruder is on your premises. These images and video streams can also be directed to your smart phone.

Please note that monthly subscriptions may be required for some services such as storing large amounts of IP camera video footage off site.

STEP 2
Adding Lighting Control to your HA 2.0 System

Lighting is a key HA 2.0 application that will benefit you in your day-to-day living by improving convenience, comfort and peace of mind! Automating your home lighting is a great way of getting started with HA 2.0.

STEP 3
Adding Heating & Smart Energy Control to your HA 2.0 System

Smart thermostats are used to control your heating and cooling systems. These thermostats are typically interfaced with your home automation controller wirelessly or via Cat6 cabling infrastructure. The ability to remotely monitor energy usage is another important function of HA 2.0 systems.

Part 2: Three 'Nice to Have' Home Automation Functions

Once you have the serious stuff done in Part I, then you might want to go on and consider extending your system to encompass three 'nice to have' features in your home.

These features are represented graphically in Figure 1.4 and described below:

❏ **Figure 1.4 – Three 'Nice to Have' Home Automation Functions**

STEP 4

Adding Multi-Room Music to your HA 2.0 System

Wired and wireless whole house audio systems offer people the ability to distribute high quality music throughout the entire home. A multi-room music system is built with the following elements:

- In-ceiling or in-wall speakers

- A multi-zone amplifier

- An interface such as an iPhone, iPad or Android device

STEP 5

Adding Whole House HDTV Distribution to your HA 2.0 System

You will need to purchase one of the following devices in order to distribute HDTV movies and TV shows to different rooms in your home, namely:

- HDMI Switch: This piece of equipment allows you to connect between one and four HDTV sources to a single TV or projector.

- HDMI Splitter: A splitter allows you to send HDMI signals from one source to multiple TV screens.

- HDMI matrix: An HDMI matrix allows you to watch any HDTV source on any TV!

STEP 6

Adding a Home Cinema to your HA 2.0 System

The following components are required to build a full-blown home theatre surround sound system:

- An AV receiver

- Suitable cabling

- Speakers

- A sub-woofer

- A TV display or projector

- A Wi-Fi to IR extender

The combination of all these components together will allow you to enjoy the cinema experience at home.

Each of the steps associated with parts I and II are explained in the following chapters.

Things to Remember:

In this chapter you were introduced to HA 2.0; here are the key take away points to remember:

- We are at the beginning of a new era in the home technology industry – Home Automation 2.0 (HA 2.0).

- What most people don't realize is that the addition of an automation system to your home is surprisingly affordable, easy to install and use.

- Over the past couple of years, energy management and security have become key drivers of the global home automation industry.

- HA 2.0 systems help to increase your security, save money and improve comfort levels on a daily basis.

- The functionality of your home automation system will keep expanding over the years. To get you going start small with a HA 2.0 controller and a couple of modules.

Now that you understand what Home Automation 2.0 is, associated benefits and a broad outline of what's required, you're now ready to move on to picking a technology platform for building your new HA 2.0 system.

Okay, ready for some Techie Talk!

CHAPTER 2

CHOOSING A HA 2.0 TECHNOLOGY PLATFORM

As with any emerging industry, a number of standards are competing to become the de-facto HA 2.0 technology platform. There is a lot at stake and it is important you have a very general understanding of the different platforms as it has an impact on the types of products available for future expansion of your system.

In this chapter we discuss the four most popular technologies used by HA 2.0 systems, namely structured wiring, Z-Wave, Insteon, and Zigbee.

What is a Structured House Wiring System?

> **❝** *A home built with structured wiring supports all existing home technologies as well as technologies that come available in the future.* **❞**

Conventional wiring systems are adequate for basic voice and fax communications but are unable to support the very latest home technologies like high-speed Internet access, home theatre, distributed audio, automation and lighting control systems.

As a result of the inadequacies of conventional wiring systems, a new technique for pre-wiring a house has become the de-facto way to cable a new building. The technique is called 'structured wiring' and is emerging as a standard way of wiring all new houses in the future. So what is structured wiring?

Structured wiring is a generic term used to describe how to wire your house with an organized cabling system that is capable of distributing a variety of signals throughout a house. The term 'organized' in this context means that each point on the network is wired back directly with individual cables to a centralized box.

A home built with structured wiring supports all existing home technologies as well as technologies that come available in the future.

Benefits of Structured Wiring Systems

There are some clear advantages to wiring your home in a structured manner for both the builder and the homebuyer. Table 2.1 below illustrates the key advantages of installing a structured wiring system.

❑ **Table 2.1 – Key Advantages of Structured Wiring Systems**

Home Buyers	Increased resale value to your home
	Improved convenience
	Enhanced aesthetics and appearance
	Pre-wiring during construction does not cost an awful lot
Builders	Additional revenue stream
	Improved competitive edge
	Problems that can affect services such as phone, TV and broadband are isolated to a single cable

A correctly installed structured wiring system is considered a permanent feature of your house and increases its sale value if you ever want to sell in the future.

The installation of a structured wiring system provides the bandwidth and in-home distribution for such services as:

- Whole-House High-Speed Internet Access
- Whole-House HDTV & 3D Entertainment
- Home Computer Networking
- Whole-House Music
- In-Home Camera Monitoring
- Home Automation and Control

Installing a Structured Wiring System

Installing structured wiring in a home creates what is commonly referred to as a home network. Here are six specific sequential steps that you need to do when installing a new wiring system to support various HA 2.0 sub-systems:

STEP 1   **Define your Requirements**

The first step is to define the types of functionality required in the various rooms of your home. For instance, in the main bathroom you may only want a couple of in-ceiling speakers for background music; whereas in the living room you may want to install a sophisticated home theatre and lighting control system.

STEP 2   **Create a Room-by-Room Wiring Schedule**

Your next step is to create a detailed wiring schedule to future proof your new home or extension for a range of next generation HA 2.0 applications. The cabling schedule itself should be in list format and include details such as:

① Some type of numbering system to identify each cable.

② The type of cable – speaker, Cat5e, Cat6, HDMI or coaxial.

③ From and 'to' locations – from a centralized area to a particular room.

④ Backbox requirements – US, British or EU style backboxes

⑤ The purpose of the cable – i.e. video surveillance.

> **! Quick Side Note from Gerard:**
> Don't forget your Power Requirements!

STEP 3   **Install a Structured Wiring Box**

When wiring a house for home networking services, most experts (that includes me ☺) will recommend a solution, which includes a centralized structured wiring box that is interconnected to various rooms through a series of Cat 5 and RG-6 bundled cables. Structured wiring boxes, also called structured wiring panels or distribution cabinets cost very little and are located at a central location where all your wires are run back to. It is a standalone piece of equipment that acts as a centralized point for your home network.

Generally, a structured wiring box is made of metal (plastic models are also available) and houses various music, phone, TV and home network distribution modules. There are a number of different structured wiring enclosure sizes available on the market. The size of the enclosure is determined by how many distribution modules you plan on using. As a basic guide you should use a 12" enclosure for 2 hubs, a 14" enclosure for 3 to 4 hubs, and a 28" enclosure for anything more. The above suggestions should give you enough room to not only accommodate various phone, data, TV and whole house music modules but also provide space for the various runs of cables inside the box.

Where should I locate my new structured wiring box?

First and foremost you need to identify a dry and cool part of your home for installing a structured wiring box. Most people locate in the utility room, in the basement, or even under the stairs. Please avoid the attic as they get too hot during the summer months and cold during the winter period. Locating the wiring box in a central location is also good practice as it cuts down the length of your cable runs and of course the box needs to be accessible. So if you're getting sick of looking at that bundle of cables under the stairs or in the utility, then why not buy a structured wiring box and a couple of modules and start to build out a wired based home network.

STEP 4 **Run Cables and Wires**

The wires included in a structured wiring system may vary by installation but will nearly always include coaxial cable and high-grade category 5, 5e, or 6 cabling. The coaxial cable handles the TV distribution throughout the home whilst the category 5e cable carries computer and telephone signals. To simplify installations some cable manufacturers have bundled both cable types together and covered with a strong plastic coating. These bundles usually consist of two category 5e cables and two coaxial cables. So rather than running multiple cable runs to each outlet a single bundle is run through the walls of the new house and terminated at the wall outlet. Note that speaker cable is also frequently installed to support multi-zone music systems. All of the wires are run between the outlets and the distribution box in a star like fashion. Using the star topology is more efficient and reliable than the traditional approach to wiring a house.

Figure 2.1 illustrates a star type topology completed during the 'Celtic Tiger' years here in Ireland for an apartment block in the centre of Cork City – the real capital of Ireland ☺

❑ **Figure 2.1 Star Wiring Topology for Cork Digital Apartments**

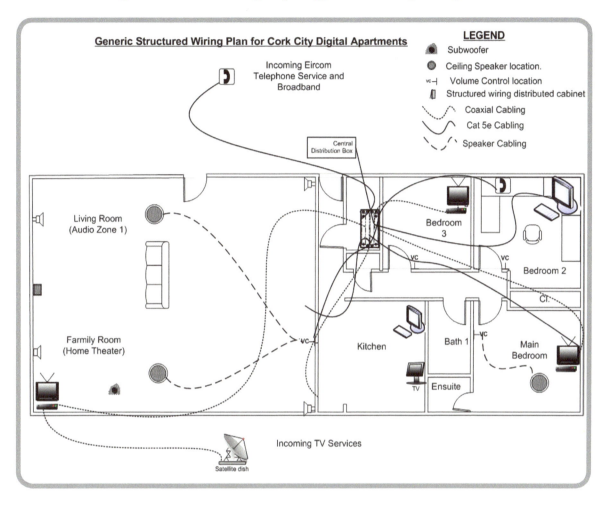

Please also note that labels for each of the cables should be applied during this step.

STEP 5 Install Multi-purpose Wall Plates & Terminate Cables

The next step in the implementation of a fully operational structured wiring system is to install some multi-purpose wall plates. A multi-purpose outlet comprises of two elements – connectors and a wall plate. Each outlet can be customized to your specific needs based on which services are desired in each room. For example a home office will require a multi-purpose outlet that supports broadband connectivity and telephone connectivity. Proper termination of cables is vital for effective communication.

STEP 6 Install HA 2.0 Centralized Modules

Once the structured wiring box is installed, it is time to start thinking about laying out the home networking components that you plan to install inside the box. As a rule of thumb you should consider mounting devices like telephone and CAT5e patch panels into the upper part of the box, whereas active devices such as network switches, routers, music servers and video amplifiers are normally mounted in the middle area. You need to also ensure that there is adequate spacing between devices to allow for air-flow for cooling purposes. The bottom section of the cabinet is typically reserved for power and expansion purposes.

A basic module layout that supports broadband, phone and TV services in a two-bedroom London apartment is presented in the diagram below.

❑ **Figure 2.2 – Customised layout plan to support basic communications services**

If you are currently building a house or an extension, then it costs relatively little to install a structured wiring system and use as a platform to build your HA 2.0 automation system.

As a rule of thumb, if you can wire, your first choice should be a wired network. If however you are like most of us and your home was not built with a structured wiring system, then there are three awesome wireless HA 2.0 technologies to choose from – Z-Wave, INSTEON and Zigbee.

What is Z-Wave?

As the name implies Z-wave is a wireless home control technology that is retrofit-able into existing homes. In other words there is no need to chase walls, drill ceilings or rip up carpets. From a technical standpoint, Z-Wave consists of low power radio waves that travel through the walls and floors of your house.

Z-Wave is owned by Sigma Designs and has slowly been building momentum over the past three years – as of 2012 over 200 manufacturers from around the world have embedded Z-Wave chips into electronic devices ranging from thermostats and lighting switches to alarm sensors and flood detection units. Once an electronic device has been engineered to include a Z-Wave chipset, it becomes part of the Z-Wave ecosystem and is able to communicate with hundreds of other Z-Wave certified devices on the marketplace today.

Z-wave devices can be used to control a plethora of functions within your home all from iOS, Windows 8 and Android smartphones or tablets.

Benefits for Homeowners

Z-Wave is simple to install – No electrician required for most Z-Wave installations. The majority of the devices are either pluggable or battery operated. Once your Z-Wave device is unpacked, it's simply a matter of tapping a button and enrolling the device into your existing Z-Wave network.

Z-Wave is expandable – Z-Wave lets you build your control system as your needs grow. As an example, some people start with a basic security Z-Wave kit comprising of an automation controller, a couple of Z-Wave door contacts, one or two pluggable Z-Wave dimmers and a Wi-Fi camera. Once people get comfortable with this setup, they often start to build out their Z-Wave network through the addition of various other types of Z-Wave devices.

Z-Wave Is Affordable – Yes Z-Wave is really cheap when compared to professionally installed home control systems. Z-Wave makes home automation accessible to the mass market. Products are widely available to buy from a variety of online shops.

Z-wave is Reliable – When used for serious applications such as protecting, heating and providing lights in your home, wireless protocols such as Z-Wave need to be reliable and capable of operating all of the time. For instance, when you arm a Z-Wave based alarm system upon leaving in the morning, you want to be sure that the various Z-Wave sensors are notified of the change in status. Z-wave provides such reliability if correctly installed and configured.

Z-Wave takes Safety into Account – Z-Wave devices are used in family environments, thus electronic radio emissions from items such as light switches and thermostats are kept to a minimum, typically less than 10 milli-watts (mW). This level of power only gets applied when communication occurs between sensors and the HA controller. This burst of communication occurs infrequently and during a very short period of time, typically micro-seconds. In addition to low transmission power levels, Z-Wave devices are normally installed at least a meter away from family members, which again dilutes the levels of exposure to an extent that Z-Wave poses no safety risk to people.

Z-wave is secure – Z-Wave includes various security mechanisms that guarantee against un-authorized third parties interfering with your in-home control network.

Z-Wave products are easy to use – One of the main functions of any HA 2.0 system is to make life easier for occupants. Z-wave was designed from the ground up to reduce the complications associated with modern day living.

Z-Wave is interoperable – With Z-Wave you can expand your HA 2.0 system on a phased basis over time. As your system grows, it is likely that you will be installing products from different vendors. Z-wave provides a platform, which provides interoperability between several manufacturers.

Z-Wave provides good coverage in your home – Z-wave **comes with in-built intelligence that** allows mains powered Z-Wave modules such as plug-in smart plugs and wall light switches to repeat a signal once received. For example, if the range of the signal from your home automation controller is approximately 30 metres, Z-wave provides for routing through a maximum of 4 separate Z-Wave devices; thus the maximum Z-Wave range is approximately 120 metres. In other words Z-Wave devices work as a team!

Z-Wave is an international standard – Z-Wave is now officially an International Telecommunication Union (ITU) standard. Z-Wave uses the ISM (industrial, scientific, and medical) frequency band in Europe which is fixed at 868.42 and approx 900Mhz in the USA and elsewhere.

Although Z-wave boasts a ton of benefits, the only real drawback from a high level perspective is its 'proprietary nature' – there are only one or two companies making the chips for Z-Wave product manufacturers.

From an end user perspective, that has little or no consequence when deciding to install a HA 2.0 system!

Z-Wave Product Categories

Table 2.2 provides a brief explanation of the various types of product categories used to build HA 2.0 systems.

❏ **Table 2.2 – Summary of different Z-Wave product categories**

Product Category	Description
Light switches and dimmers	Available in four form factors: Dimmable plug in modules for wall outlets ON/OFF plug-in modules for wall outlets Traditional wall replacement switches Micro-switches.
Load control modules	Generally available as plug in modules or hardwired versions.
Blind control modules	Available in two form factors: Replacement for traditional wall switches Micro-switches that work with existing wall switches
Environmental sensors	Z-Wave enabled temperature, humidity, flood, and carbon monoxide sensors are all available.
Sirens	Z-Wave sirens are an important part of a wireless Z-Wave home automated alarm system.
Heating controls	TRVs (Thermostat Radiator Valves) and thermostats are used to interface with your in-home heating system.
Security & Alarms	Door locks, sirens, IP cameras, alarm systems, presence detectors, window, & door contacts help to ensure that all areas of your home are protected against intruders.
Handheld Remote controls	Available in different form factors ranging from basic hard button remotes to high-end universal remote controls that include an LCD screen.
Home controllers	A number of manufacturers are selling home controllers that provide varying levels of functionalities when it comes to controlling and managing your home.

How Z-Wave works?

The sections below give a brief overview of how Z-Wave works when installed in your home.

Components of an End-to-End Z-Wave System

A typical Z-Wave based automation systems uses two device types to wirelessly control your house:

 Controllers – As the name implies a controller is used to manage and control other Z-Wave devices, also known as slaves. There are two main types of controllers, namely portable and static.

- Portable controllers are as the name suggests, mobile. A remote control with hard buttons is an example of a portable Z-wave controller. Although portable Z-Wave controllers are easy to use they can be prone to getting lost behind the couch or in the play room from time to time ☺

- Static controllers are mains powered, positioned in a fixed location in your home and connected to a broadband router. Examples of static Z-Wave controllers, include:

  - A USB key connected to a PC

  - A software application running on your home PC

  - A dedicated Z-Wave gateway device

> **! Quick Side Note from Gerard:**
>
> Wherever you live in the world, make sure that whatever Z-Wave products you buy online operate in your local Z-Wave approved frequency band.

Slaves – These hardware modules provide a limited but important role in the day to day running of your HA 2.0 network. Although they are unable to initiate communications with a controller, they do provide vital information such as status, temperature, humidity, light level data when polled by the controller. Similar to controllers, slaves are also classified as follows:

- *Battery operated slaves* which turn on radio communication periodically for short periods of time at specific intervals in order to communicate with its controller. When radio communication is not needed they will turn the radio off to conserve battery life. Door and window sensors are examples of Z-Wave battery operated slaves.

- *Mains powered slaves* have a slight advantage over battery operated slaves in the sense that they are in active mode all of the time and are able to re-transmit messages to other devices on the Z-Wave network – thus improving coverage

Z-Wave Routing

Z-Wave uses a mesh network architecture; in other words it is able to circumvent radio dead spots by redirecting a signal to its destination Z-Wave devices through a number of intermediate devices.

A simple example of how Z-Wave routes signals is illustrated in Figure 2.3. If an automation controller wants to send an OFF command to a Z-Wave light switch in the garage and it is out of range of the controller, then Z-Wave will create a route through the network (via the pluggable unit), which will ensure that the command reaches the light switch.

! Quick Side Note from • Gerard:

Tapping a button on your Z-Wave slave device forces the unit to wake up immediately and start communicating with your HA 2.0 controller. Useful if you need to verify that a particular sensor is working correctly.

❑ **Figure 2.3 Simple example of how Z-Wave routes signals**

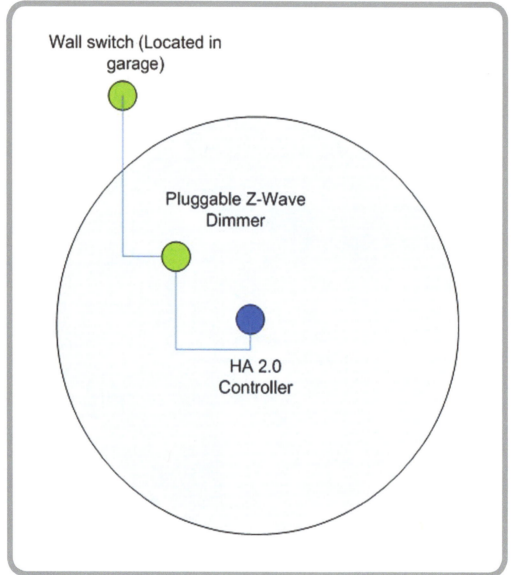

It is important to note again that the ability to repeat and re-route signals around a building is limited to Z-Wave devices that are powered by the mains electrical supply. Battery operated devices (typically in sleep mode) are not designed as repeaters! Smart Z-Wave pluggable units are often used to improve Z-Wave coverage in a house or business.

In addition to the mesh architecture, Z-Wave devices use two-way communication methods. All Z-wave home automation controllers and devices are two-way. From a technical perspective this means that the home controller receives acknowledgements and status updates once communication is taking place over your Z-Wave network.

❑ Figure 2.4 Z-Wave 2-Way Capabilities

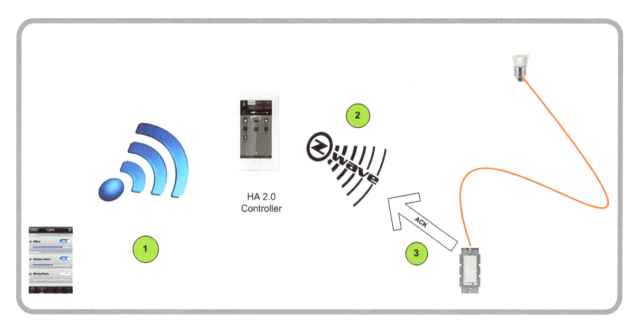

For instance, if you consider the simple example illustrated in Figure 2.4 of an iPhone turning ON the kitchen Z-Wave light switch, the following steps are initiated:

①   This command gets sent over the Wi-Fi network to your Z-wave home automation controller.

②   The Z-wave home automation controller in turns issues the TURN ON command over a Z-Wave network to the in-wall Z-Wave light switch dimmer located in the kitchen.

③   The Z-Wave dimmer switch turns on the light and returns an acknowledgement to your home automation controller.

Sending a command from your iPhone or Android device and getting a result (i.e. the light turns ON) typically takes between 40 and 60 milliseconds.

How Z-Wave Devices 'Talk' To Each Other

As with all networking systems, commands are used by different devices on a Z-Wave network to communicate with each other. In total there are over 50 different types of commands supported by Z-Wave. Rather than covering all fifty in this e-book, the three most used commands are described below and illustrated as an example in Figure 2.5.

SET – This command is accompanied with a value of between 0 and 255. So in this example the light switch will turn ON when it receives a 255 and OFF when it receives a 0.

GET – This command is used to ask a Z-Wave device for a value. In this example the command is sent from the controller to request a report about the switching state.

REPORT – The response to the GET command is called a REPORT and is typically a value of between 0 and 255. In this case the Z-Wave switch reports a 255 value, which tells the controller that the switch is ON.

❑ **Figure 2.5 Z-Wave command execution examples**

SET=➜255

Light turns On

GET=000

Light On

REPORT = 255

Light On

Z-Wave Addressing

The Z-Wave protocol defines two addressing identifiers, namely Home and Node IDs. The following table summarizes both of these parameters.

❑ **Table 2.3 - Z-Wave Addressing Characteristics**

Z-wave Identifier	Characteristics
Home ID	The Home ID identifier is built in at the factory. It is 4 bytes in length. HA 2.0 controllers have their own Home ID – Slaves do not. The Home ID gets assigned to Z-Wave modules that get added to the network.
Node ID	The node ID is assigned by the HA 2.0 controller. The HA 2.0 controller has its own Node ID. It is possible to have 256 Node IDs (Maximum capacity of Z-Wave network).

To understand Z-Wave addressing in a better way let's consider the simple example in Figure 2.6. In this case, the Z-Wave thermostat and door contact have no Home ID before they are configured on the Z-Wave network. Once these devices are setup they are assigned both a Home ID and a unique node ID that allows them to operate as part of the Z-Wave based home control network.

❑ **Figure 2.6 Z-Wave addressing example**

Installing a Z-wave HA 2.0 System

Installing a Z-Wave based HA 2.0 system consists of three separate steps:

STEP 1
Identify a suitable physical location for your HA 2.0 controller

You need to locate the controller in close proximity to mains power and reasonably central in your property if at all possible. It is recommended that the distance between your new controller and each of the Z-Wave modules should not exceed 25 meters.

You also need to be cognizant that obstacles, electromagnetic noise and mounting location can undermine your installation and cause issues further down the road. A brief explanation of these three issues is provided below:

Issue 1: Obstacles causing signal loss

Obstacles such as furniture, walls and doors all help to weaken the signal between the controller and the various modules. The following table shows the affects that different obstacles have on a Z-wave signal strength.

❑ **Table 2.4 – Z-Wave Signal Reduction Characteristics of Various Obstacle Types**

Obstacle Type	Signal reduction
Concrete Walls	Signal reduction is approximately 30%
Timber Walls, furniture and doors	Signal reduction is approximately 10%
Windows/Glass	Signal reduction is approximately 10%

The effects of obstacles on signal strength are explained by the following example.

❏ Figure 2.7 Signal Loss Example Calculation

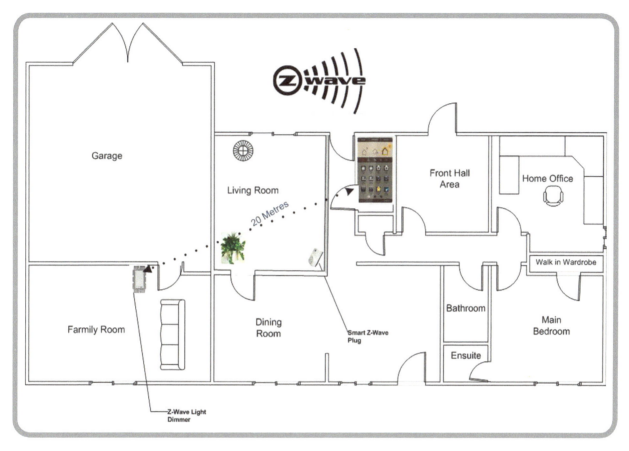

As illustrated in Figure 2.7 – suppose you have an installed HA 2.0 controller and a Z-Wave light switch 20 meters apart. There are two walls between the devices, made of different material types, namely a studded wall and a block wall. Table 2.5 calculates the signal loss caused by the two walls.

❏ Table 2.5 – Example Calculation to Measure Signal Loss as a Result of Obstacles

Obstacle 1 - a block wall	Knocks 30 percent off the range – Down to 14 metres
Obstacle 2 - a slab wall	Another 10% knocked off the range – Down to 12.6 metres.
Obstacle 3 (Plants and furniture)	Down to 10 metres!

You also need to take into account other factors such as plants and furniture when estimating signal range. It now appears that the operational range of the Z-Wave signal is 10 meters rather than 20 meters as originally expected. The solution is to either extend signal range by adding a Z-Wave plug-in module to the network or else move the controller closer to the light switch.

Issue 2: Noise Interference

Try and locate your Z-wave modules at least 50 cm away from pieces of equipment that generate interference such as computers, cordless phones, the microwave in the kitchen, electrical motors and fluorescent lamps.

Issue 3: Mounting locations

Common sense is required when it comes to mounting sensors. For instance, if you are mounting a motion detector on your outside wall then you need to attach the sensor to the wall in a location that does not completely destroy the Z-wave signal originating from your Z-Wave controller.

For example, if, as is the case for most installs, you need to mount a motion detector at roof or indeed ceiling level, make sure you position the sensor slightly underneath the floor or ceiling level. As shown in Figure 2.8, if you mount the sensor in-line with the floor level then the Z-Wave radio signal will need to penetrate dense concrete or metal structures. This will be ineffective and lead to high signal attenuation levels.

Figure 2.8 – Mounting location considerations

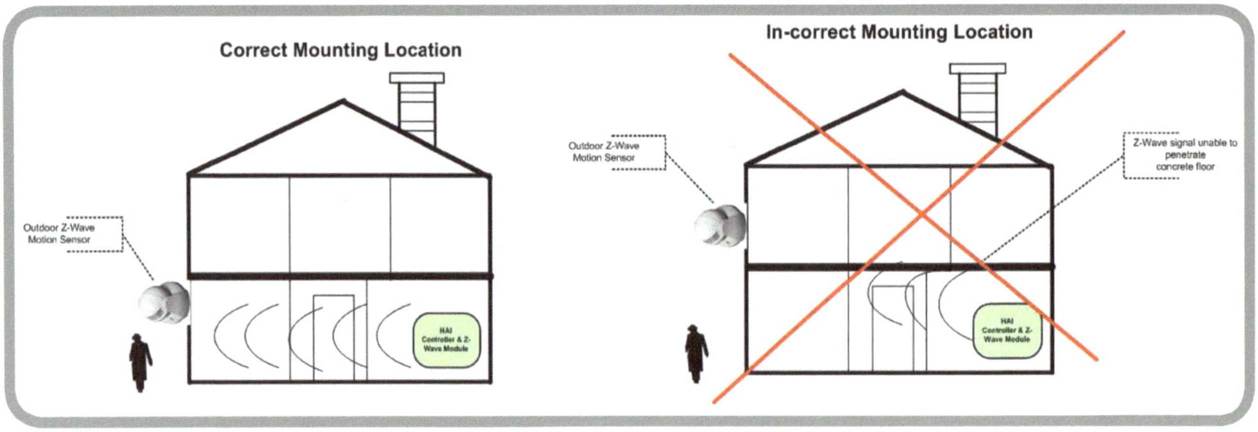

![Figure 2.8 showing correct and incorrect mounting locations for outdoor Z-Wave motion sensors on a house]

STEP 2   Powering and Wiring Z-Wave Hardware Modules

In general, powering and connecting up the various Z-Wave components is pretty straight forward. **The following table summarizes what's required.**

❑ **Table 2.6 - Z-Wave Physical Connections**

Z-Wave Component	Power up and Wiring Tasks	Install Expertise Required
Z-Wave controllers	Plug controller into mains and patch a Cat5 cable into the broadband router from the automation controller.	None
Z-Wave wall light switches and micro-switches	Turn power off at main circuit board and then install light switch.	Need to be comfortable working with mains power cabling. May require the services of an electrical contractor.
Z-Wave door, window , and motion sensors	Insert batteries and attach to relevant areas.	The only expertise required is common sense! For instance, if motion detectors need to be mounted, then locate at an appropriate height to pick up movement.
Plug-in lamp modules	Plug module into mains powered socket.	None
Z-Wave door locks	Retrofitting existing door lock	Probably requires a door lock specialist installer.
Z-Wave thermostats and thermostatic radiator valve (TRVs)	Thermostats and TRVs need to be interconnected with your heating system.	Most people have limited expertise when it comes to in-home boiler systems. A HVAC contractor may be required to retrofit these hardware modules into your home.
Blind control modules	Typically involves elements of cabling and possibly working with high voltage switches.	Need to be comfortable working with mains power cabling. May require the services of an electrical contractor.
Environmental sensors	Similar to alarm sensors – batteries provide the required power to operate.	None

STEP 3   Configuring Z-Wave modules on your HA 2.0 Controller

There are two primary configuration operations that you need to be aware of when building a Z-Wave based automation – *Inclusion* and *Exclusion*.

 Inclusion

Every Z-Wave network consists of a home automation controller and one or more slave devices or receivers. There is an upper limit of 254 devices per Z-Wave network; not likely to be exceeded in a typical installation :-)

Extra devices can be added to the network at any stage. The technical terms typically used to add devices to a Z-Wave network are "inclusion" or "pairing". The process of inclusion commences when the automation controller is put into inclusion mode; this is typically done via a software interface or by simply pressing a button on your controller. The Z-Wave slave device is also put into inclusion mode by tapping a physical button on the unit itself. Once this occurs and both devices are in include mode then some protocol handshaking takes place along with the following actions:

- Details of other Z-Wave devices that are in direct wireless range are sent to the HA 2.0 controller.

- The information gathered during the inclusion process is used to build a new routing table or to update an existing one.

- The binary number '1' is used to indicate Z-Wave neighboring devices that are in direct wireless range of each other. Table 2.7 shows an example of a routing table created during a recent installation.

❑ **Table 2.7 – Example Z-Wave routing table**

	HA 2.0 Controller	Kitchen pluggable Lamp	Dining room wall switch	Front door contact	Back door contact	Hall Motion Sensor
HA 2.0 Controller	0	1	1	1	0	1
Kitchen Pluggable Lamp	1	0	1	0	1	1
Dining room wall switch	1	1	0	0	0	1
Front door contact	0	1	1	0	0	1
Back door contact	1	1	0	0	0	0
Hall Motion Sensor	1	0	1	1	1	0

! Quick Side Note from Gerard:

One task that occurs during inclusion is the measurement by the HA 2.0 controller of Z-Wave signal strength; thus Z-Wave devices should be installed at their final physical locations during the inclusion process. There are one or two HA 2.0 controller manufacturers who accommodate this configuration requirement by supplying a portable battery as part of your purchase.

Once the above inclusion process is completed, the Z-wave devices start to communicate with each other from that moment on!

This process gets repeated for each new device that gets added to your internal Z-Wave home network.

As shown in Figure 2.9 there is also an element of software configuration that forms part of the inclusion process.

❑ Figure 2.9 – Adding Z-Wave products to your HA 2.0 Network

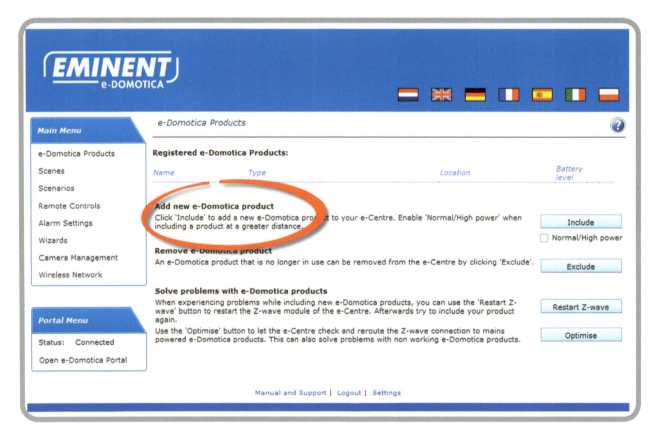

  Exclusion

In the world of Z-Wave, disconnecting a device is called "exclusion". The process of excluding Z-Wave devices is pretty much the reverse of inclusion and consists of a series of button presses and taps.

What is INSTEON?

" *Many of the benefits associated with Z-Wave HA 2.0 systems are mirrored with the INSTEON range of products* "

INSTEON is new to us here in Europe! INSTEON was developed by a division of SmartLabs Inc based in the USA, Similar to Z-Wave, INSTEON is also used to automate a range of functions within your home ranging from alarms to lighting and heating.

Benefits to Homeowners

Many of the benefits associated with Z-Wave HA 2.0 systems are mirrored with the INSTEON range of products:

- **Reliable:** INSTEON uses both Powerline and airwaves to communicate messages, which helps to maximize reliability for this technology.

- **Fast response levels:** Speaking from personal experience, the time taken between tapping my iPhone and getting a response from an INSTEON enabled lighting control module is negligible. Apparently commands can activate devices in fractions of a second, making the time delay negligible to the human eye.

- **It's easy to install:** This obviously depends on the type of product you are installing – for instance, connecting in a lighting control smart plug to an INSTEON network will be less involved than retro-fitting a wall light switch. There is however no enrolment process, which can save time and simplify the installation process.

- **X-10 compatibility:** For the general population, compatibility with a HA 1.0 standard called X-10 is of little consequence, however it is a useful feature for those of us who have purchased X10 modules in the past.

How INSTEON Works?

Overall, INSTEON operates in a similar manner to Z-Wave. There are however, some unique techniques used by this technology, which are briefly described in the sections below.

Components of an end-to-end INSTEON system

All INSTEON products can assume any one of the following roles:

Controllers are responsible for sending messages.

Responders receive automation messages.

Repeaters are responsible for receiving and resending messages on the INSTEON network. INSTEON devices are automatically enabled as repeaters when they are connected into your electrical wiring system. Please note that battery operated INSTEON modules do not act as repeaters to conserve battery power.

Utilizes both airwaves and high voltage cabling to send and receive commands

As mentioned briefly above, INSTEON uses a dual mesh approach, which basically means it uses both airwaves and high voltage cabling simultaneously to provide communication between devices. This reduces dependency on one or the other media, which is good from a reliability standpoint. So if there is a power outage then wireless acts as a backup and vice versa.

Command messages are propagated using a mechanism called simulcasting

Unlike Z-Wave, INSTEON does not use routing as a means of sending commands around the network. Instead it uses a simpler approach called simulcasting, which basically means that multiple INSTEON devices are sending the exact same command message. This helps to increase signal strength and eliminates the need to know the topology of the network.

A process called 'Statelink' is used

This mechanism, which is unique to INSTEON, recalls a previous state of a module, rather than using specific commands.

INSTEON module addressing

INSTEON assigns a unique ID to each module during manufacturing. This in turn becomes the permanent address when installed in your home.

INSTEON Product Categories

INSTEON has built up a nice portfolio of HA 2.0 installable products over the years, including:

- Software and computer controllers

- Light dimmers & switches

- Handheld & tabletop remotes

- Plug-in modules

- Thermostats

- Sprinkler control

- Alarm sensors

- Energy monitoring devices

Although confined to the US market, many of the above products are now starting to become available here in Europe, Australia and New Zealand. In fact, I tested many of the EU compliant INSTEON products before they became commercially available.

Installing an INSTEON HA 2.0 System

As described earlier, installation is genuinely easy for modules such as the smart plugs, alarm sensors, and basic controllers. Physical installation will involve one of the following actions:

- Plugging-In – For some INSTEON modules installation will be as simple as plugging a module into the wall. The only gotcha is that you have the correct plug adapter for your country.

- Wiring-in – Wiring devices such as INSTEON light switches is easy for a DIY person. If however you are not comfortable with working on high voltage circuits then serious consideration needs to be given to getting a 'handyman' or an electrical contractor to deal with wiring your INSTEON modules.

- Inserting Batteries – Adding batteries and mounting on a wall or ceiling is pretty much all that is required in this instance.

There are two options for getting INSTEON modules to connect and communicate with each other:

 OPTION 1: Linking between both modules is achieved by simply pressing and holding a button on each module for a couple of seconds.

 OPTION 2: Use a software program to connect the various INSTEON modules with each other.

It is also important to note signal strength and reliability increases exponentially through the addition of extra INSTEON devices. So the more INSTEON devices you have on your new HA 2.0 network the better.

What is Zigbee?

It is beyond our scope in this e-book to provide a comprehensive technical description of Zigbee; but certain aspects of this emerging technology are covered in the sections below.

To start with, Zigbee is an open public standard for wireless sensor networking that is developed by the Zigbee alliance. The technology was originally created under the brand name HomeRF back in the late nineties. Ironically, I devoted a full chapter to Home RF in an earlier book that I released in 1999 titled 'The Essential Guide to Home Networking'!

Zigbee supports some notable features:

- *Utilizes a mesh networking topology* – The radio mesh networking topology used by Zigbee provides for high levels of reliability.

- *Smart grid integration* – Zigbee is optimized for smart metering applications. In fact it has become the defacto standard for the utility industry.

- *Low power consumption* – Power consumption for Zigbee products is quite low – battery life can last up to two years for most installs.

Wide range of applications – Both Insteon and Z-Wave are very much HA 2.0 application centric, whereas Zigbee has a much wider reach and is also used in the following areas:

- Industrial control

- Commercial building energy management systems

- Medical & healthcare applications

- Remote controls for managing A/V equipment

Operating frequencies – Zigbee operates at 2.4GHz worldwide, 915 MHz in the US or 868 MHz in Europe.

Interoperable – Once the correct hardware gateways are used, Zigbee can co-exist with other HA 2.0 platforms such as Insteon and Z-Wave.

Zigbee Product Categories

As of this writing, the range of Zigbee products available to homeowners is quite limited. Most of the products, typically available through professional digital integrators or utility companies are primarily used for energy management purposes.

The following table summarizes currently available Zigbee enabled smart energy products:

❑ **Table 2.8 – Zigbee Enabled Smart Energy Product Categories**

Product Category	Description
Programmable thermostats	Optimized for smart grid projects, Zigbee thermostats provide temperature control over Heating & Air Conditioning (HVAC) systems.
In-home displays	When integrated with a smart grid, these Zigbee enabled displays allow utility customers to track their energy usage in chart or graph form.
Load Control Modules	These modules are typically smart grid enabled and allow homeowners to manage high energy consumption appliances such as washing machines and boiler pumps.
Lighting switches and dimmers	Zigbee embedded switches and dimmers are typically used to build a lighting control system.

When the products described above are combined with a Zigbee smart meter than the following benefits are realized:

- Energy consumption and costs becomes controllable and manageable on an App.

- Homeowners have real time access on their smartphones or tablets to gas, electricity and water usage.

- Customers can adjust their consumption patterns and avail of low cost off peak usage rates.

At the moment the choice of Zigbee products available limits your ability to build a full HA 2.0 system. You will also find that products from different manufacturers are not compatible with each other!

If however your interest in automation is confined to energy management then Zigbee provides an elegant solution that you could expand once the technology becomes more pervasive in the HA 2.0 space.

Other HA 2.0 Platforms

As is the case with any industry sector, a bunch of standards have emerged over the years. Here are three of the most popular ones:

① **X-10 –** Available since the late nineties, X-10 based devices use domestic 220V or 110V mains power wiring to communicate. Although X-10 is installed in millions of homes worldwide, issues such as interference, bandwidth limitations and lack of two way communication has hampered mainstream adoption of this HA 1.0 platform.

② **Wi-Fi –** Strictly speaking Wi-Fi is not considered a home automation communications protocol. However, it plays an important role in HA 2.0 systems because it is used to send video streams from IP cameras back to your HA controller.

③ **Enocean –** is a wireless technology that is promoted and developed by a group of companies that include some high profile names such as Siemens and Honeywell. The main selling point of Enocean is that it harvests energy from the surrounding environment and negates the need for batteries and mains power. The fact that Enocean devices, such as light switches and thermostats are self powered and easy to install, makes it a suitable technology for the HA 2.0 marketplace. In reality, Enocean products are light on the ground and are really only starting to make headway into commercial buildings. If Enocean delivers on its promises, then it could play a more central role within the HA 2.0 ecosystem.

Things to Remember

In this chapter, here are the key points to remember:

- New or renovated homes should install modern wiring systems to provide the capacity for current and future networks. This wiring system acts as the backbone of your HA 2.0 system. A typical wiring system will include RG-6 (coaxial) wire for multi room entertainment systems, CAT 5e or Cat6 wire for data and voice communications as well as special wiring for speakers, home controls etc.

- Realistically there are really only two wireless HA 2.0 platforms out there selling products, namely Z-Wave and INSTEON. I'm a big fan also of Zigbee, but the range of products that are commercially available is limited at the time of writing.

- The Z-Wave radio waves generated by your HA 2.0 controller are capable of penetrating various types of obstacles such as wall, doors, windows and furniture. These obstacles do however weaken the Z-Wave signal, and planning prior to an install is an important step.

- With its simple installation and configuration process INSTEON has succeeded in becoming a suitable option for consumers who want to install a HA 2.0 system.

Now that you know about the various options you have for building a new HA 2.0 system in your home, you're ready to start at Step 1 of the process – installing a controller and increasing security levels of your home.

Okay, let's get stuck into the next chapter!

CHAPTER 3

STEP 1: USE HA 2.0 TO ENHANCE FAMILY SAFETY & SECURITY LEVELS

Introduction

> **❝** *A fully installed HA 2.0 alarm system is a great way of providing us with some peace of mind when away from home.* **❞**

Ensuring that your home is safe, especially when crime rates are rising during these recessionary times is extremely important to most of us. Recent data shows that a robbery takes place every 15 seconds in the USA!

The repercussions of a break-in can be enormous. In addition to the damage and loss of personal items, people can often experience emotional trauma for months or indeed years after a house burglary.

In my mind burglary protection is one the most important components of a home automation system. With this functionality, a criminal is less likely to break into your home and steal your prized possessions.

A fully installed HA 2.0 alarm system is a great way of providing us with some peace of mind when away from home.

As with everything in life, we need to plan our approach to increasing security levels at home; this chapter provides some practical steps.

Home Security Planning

When planning for security around your home, start by thinking like a burglar. Begin outside,, preferably in the evening after the sun has gone down. Look for dark areas around your home. These can be used by potential intruders as hiding areas while they work their way inside. Look for any spot where you might think someone would work on entering your home, including doors, garages, and even second story windows.

All of these locations will need some type of sensor protecting them. When you add a security system, you'll need to plan for covering each of these areas.

How Home Automation 2.0 Alarm Systems Work?

Enhancing home security can be as simple as adding the following types of sensors:

- Motion – Used to detect an intruder's presence.

- Glass break – Once a window is broken the sensor sends a signal back to your HA 2.0 controller.

- Door contacts – Once armed, a signal is sent to the controller if the door is opened.

- Window contacts – Operates in a similar manner to door contacts.

These sensors are available as wired or wireless.

An example of a ground floor layout and recommended locations for different types of alarm sensors is presented in Figure 3.1.

> **! Quick Side Note from ● Gerard:**
>
> Ensure that the HA motion detector you buy is equipped with pet immunity capabilities if you own a dog or cat.

☐ **Figure 3.1 HA 2.0 alarm system – recommended sensor locations**

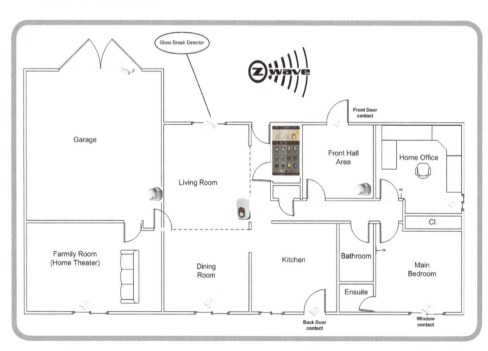

Once a sensor is tripped by a thief entering your home, a signal is sent to the home automation controller. In addition to setting off the internal siren, the controller will also send you a text message or email, informing of you of events as they unfold.

HA 2.0 alarm systems support some notable features:

- They are operated using an interface such as a touchscreen, keypad, tablet device or a smartphone.

- Highly customisable to meet your security needs – for instance with most HA 2.0 alarm systems it is up to you to decide the code, the entry delay and exit delay time periods.

- Some systems on the market also allow you to program a phone number of who will be called in case of an alarm. If you are unable to take action, if you do not answer your telephone or if the call is diverted to voice mail, most HA 2.0 products will allow you to specify who is to be called next. When professional monitoring is used, the automation controller contacts the central station, which in turn contacts the appropriate authorities.

> **!Quick Side Note from •Gerard:**
>
> During the configuration process you also need to specify what security sensors must be active.

- HA 2.0 controllers provide options for alarm settings for when you leave home (AWAY Mode) and when you go to sleep (NIGHT mode).

The types of functionality supported by HA 2.0 alarm systems include:

- The use of your HA 2.0 system to monitor, arm and disarm your in-home alarm from anywhere in the world with a smartphone or tablet.

- Disarm your security system automatically when a particular door lock code is entered.

- Arm your security system automatically when other devices are controlled.

- Receive email, text or spoken alerts when any zones are triggered.

Home Controllers Overview

Before starting to get into the 'meat and potatoes' of building out your HA 2.0 system, you will first need to choose a home automation controller.

The home automation controller is the heart of your HA 2.0 system and is typically installed at a fixed location in your house.

Home Controllers are hardware devices and available in different form factors:

- *Home automation remote controls*: Simple low level devices that look like a hand-held remote control and allow you to control a small number of devices.

- *Wired home automation controllers*: On the other end of the spectrum you have electronic circuit board type products like the HAI Lumina, that get mounted into a structured wiring distribution box. These controller types are generally installed as part of a new construction project or wiring upgrade to an existing building.

- *Cool looking home automation controllers*: If you are looking for a controller that closely resembles your cable set-top box or broadband router then the VERA3 or VERA Lite from Micasaverde and the HC2 from Fibaro are more likely to tickle your fancy.

- *Touchscreen home automation controllers*: And finally, if you want a touchscreen type interface that you can mount on the wall, then check out Eminent's recently released eCentre2.

Most of these home automation controllers provide you with the following functionalities:

- Accessibility and control by tapping icons on a touchscreen, smartphone, basic remote or tablet.

- The home automation controller will connect to a range of subsystems, namely your boiler, lights, entertainment, IP cameras, alarm, environmental sensors and high energy usage loads.

- Home automation controllers support 'scenes'. A home automation scene allows you to preset the settings of one or more devices within your home, and activate these settings with a command or event. For example, when you go to bed at night, you can tap an icon on your smartphone or iPad to automatically turn OFF all the lights, place the alarm into night mode and cut power to various appliances and TV's that might be drawing power in standby mode through the night.

Once your home automation controller has been selected, it's time to examine the various options you have in terms of configuring the controller to support different types of alarms.

HA 2.0 Alarm Types

In addition to the above, most automation systems also allow you to setup the following alarm types to protect your home:

Absence Alarms

An absence alarm is used when you leave home for a period of time, for instance heading out to work. As shown in Figure 3.2 PIN code is generally used to arm an absence alarm.

❑ **Figure 3.2 Sample Screenshot of Absence Alarm User Interface**

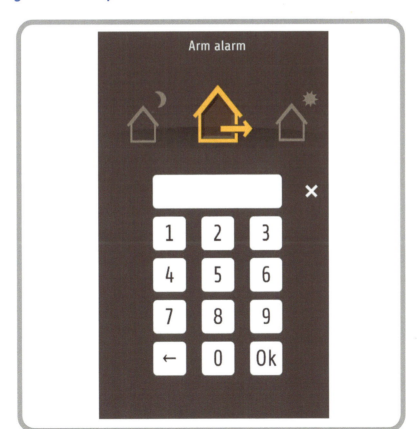

Once you have entered a correct PIN code, the various sensors around the house will be armed. As a result a break-in will initiate the following sequence of events:

① The sensors (door, window or motion) will send signals to your home automation controller.

② Your controller will activate a loud siren to make things noisy for your intruder and possibly alert a neighbour. Just makes the experience a little less enjoyable for your un-invited guest ☺

③ Depending on how you configured your system, the controller will also send you a notification text message and email.

④ If configured, your absence alarm will also start filming your intruder in action.

Night Detection Alarms

A night alarm allows you to arm specific security sensors when you go to bed. Typical configurations involve the arming of all door, window and glass break detectors. However, motion detectors that pick up movement when you go to the toilet at night are excluded from this type of configuration. This enables you or a family member to get out of bed in the middle of the night and switch on the bathroom light, but also have the alarm armed to protect against someone breaking in.

Smoke Detection Alarms

HA 2.0 enabled homes add an extra layer of safety for families through their support for smoke alarm systems that are used to detect fire and alert the occupants of the house immediately. A smoke sensor lies at the heart of your smoke alarm system and makes a loud noise once fire is detected. Additionally, it sends a signal to your home automation controller, which in turn will also make a loud noise and send an SMS, email or telephone notification to you about this alarm. It is also possible to set off various scenes once the smoke sensor is activated. For instance, you are able to configure your HA 2.0 controller to turn on certain lights in the house at a particular dim level to help your family find their way through the darkness and escape to the outside.

Here are some tips with regards to installing wireless HA 2.0 smoke alarms:

- If fire is a personal concern, then you need to consider installing a smoke alarm in each of the rooms.

- If you live in a two storey house there should be at least one smoke alarm for each floor.

As illustrated in Figure 3.3, you need to locate smoke alarms in close proximity to bedrooms.

❑ **Figure 3.3 Typical locations for Z-Wave smoke alarm units**

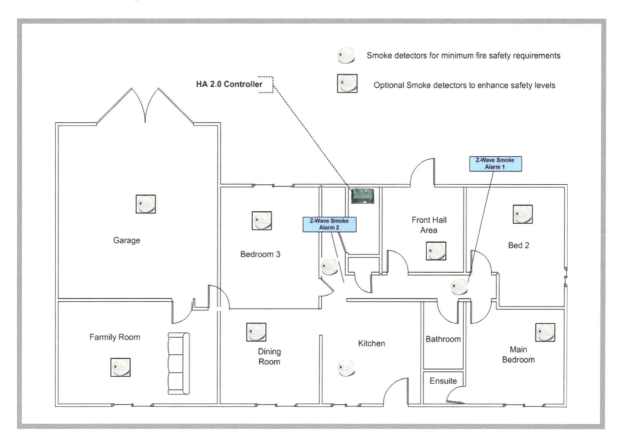

If you're interested in learning how to actually install a HA 2.0 smoke alarm system then you might want to consider enrolling in one of my video courses.

Interfacing IP Cameras with a Home Automation Controller

Before we delve into the topic of connecting an IP camera to your HA 2.0 system, let's take a minute or two to outline the main features of IP cameras:

High quality video content: IP cameras are digital and produce high-resolution video that is more accurate and clear when compared to viewing an analog video stream.

Indoor and outdoor support: Indoor IP cameras keep an eye on a particular room whereas outdoor IP cameras are weatherproof and monitor your garden or driveway.

 PoE support: Another cool feature of IP cameras is their support for a networking technology called Power over Ethernet (PoE). This technology integrates power into a standard home networking infrastructure. It enables power to be provided to the network device, such as an IP network camera, using the same cable that is used for the network connection.

> **! Quick Side Note from • Gerard:**
>
> If the camera is outside; make sure you have a Wi-Fi signal!

 PTZ support: PTZ is an abbreviation for Pan, Tilt and Zoom. As the name implies, this feature allows you to cover quite a large area and get a good overview of what is happening in your home.

 Wi-Fi support: Let's not forget about Wi-Fi; IP cameras typically provide Wi-Fi connectivity. In the context of a home automation install, Wi-Fi is the method used to stream images to an automation controller.

 Two-way audio – Some IP camera models come with a built-in microphone allowing you to listen-in to conversations and noises from intruders. In addition to a microphone, some models include an internal speaker or a line out connector that allows you to install some external speakers. Speakers allow you to issue warnings to your intruder in real time whilst he or she is up to no good in your home.

> **! Quick Side Note from • Gerard:**
>
> I would look for an IP camera that has been proven to work with a particular controller.

Now that you have zoned in on a particular IP camera make and model, the next step is to physically install and integrate with your home automation controller.

Configuring your IP camera to connect with your Controller:

For those who have limited computer or IT skills, getting an IP camera up and running can be daunting for some people. Fortunately, the cycle of getting an IP camera to send back streaming video to your iPad or smartphone is relatively straightforward. The key steps required to start using an IP camera are as follows:

STEP 1 Survey Proposed IP Camera Locations – Power and Network Connectivity

IP cameras need power and of course they need to wirelessly or over a physical wire connect to a network. The following diagram illustrates three different scenarios.

❏ **Figure 3.4 Three different wiring scenarios for IP cameras**

- *Proposed Camera Location 1:* This is easy, basically run a cable to a socket, plug in and camera communicates with HA 2.0 controller over Wi-Fi.

- *Proposed Camera Location 2:* The Wi-Fi signal is weak outside, thus a Cat5e cable needs to be run from the broadband router or network switch to this location. From a power perspective there is a mains supply nearby (outside light) and the electrician will be able to install a socket.

- *Proposed Camera Location 3:* No Wi-Fi signal or power cables nearby. Therefore, you will need to run a single Cat5e cable from the broadband router or network switch to this location and use a PoE enabled IP camera.

STEP 2   Power up and Connect Cables

As the name implies, you need to ensure that your IP camera is connected to your in-home router and the unit has power.

STEP 3   IP Camera Discovery

Once your IP camera is plugged in and the cables are connected in their correct locations, then you use a software program called a 'discovery tool' to allow your PC to access the user interface of the IP camera.

Tip: This software program is typically available on the CD that comes with your IP camera.

STEP 4   Configure Your PC on the Same Network as your IP Camera

You now need to ensure that both the PC and IP camera are on the same network. IP addresses (a globally recognised Internet numbering system for identifying electronic devices on a network) form an integral part of this step. It is therefore appropriate that we provide a brief overview of how IP addresses are structured.

An IP address is a series of four numbers separated by dots that identifies the exact physical location of a device such as an IP camera on your network. It is a 32-bit binary number. This binary number is divided into 4 groups of 8 bits ("octets"), each of which is represented by a decimal number in the range 0 to 255. The octets are separated by decimal points. An example of an IP address is 192.168.1.100

Although not evident, the IP address gets split into two separate identifiers:

① the network section is found over on the left-hand side of the number and identifies the network that the IP camera is connected to and

② the host section identifies the actual IP camera

Once the IP camera and your PC are configured on the same network, you can then use a software utility called 'Ping' to verify connectivity between both devices.

STEP 5 **Configure your IP Camera's Settings**

You are now ready to configure the camera's default settings:

● Type in the camera's IP address, a user-friendly browser-based configuration interface should appear, as shown below:

❏ **Figure 3.5 – IP Camera Home Page Example**

Depending on the type of camera, a live feed may also be available on the main home page screen.

The configurable settings will vary between IP cameras; however, here are some common ones:

- Camera parameters, including exposure, white balance, brightness, sharpness, and contrast.

- System settings such as, FTP details, motion detection and network address.

- Streaming parameters including video resolution and compression rates.

STEP 6 **Viewing the Camera on your HA 2.0 App**

Now that you can access your IP camera from a PC browser, you will no doubt aspire to viewing this video stream on your HA 2.0 app. This is a pretty easy task as long as both your IP camera and router support a technology called Universal Plug'n'Play (UPnP). Once you have confirmed that both your IP camera and router are UPnP enabled, you should in theory be able to view your IP camera over the Internet. Before attempting integration of this live feed with your HA 2.0 system, it is recommended that you verify that the camera video stream is remotely accessible by typing in the following IP address into your smartphone or PC browser:

http://External IP address of your router: port number (available in your IP camera's documentation).

There is one important observation that you need to be cognizant of when it comes to IP addresses – there are basically two types, namely static and dynamic.

> **! Quick Side Note from • Gerard:**
>
> I use 'whatsmyip. org' to identify my router's IP address.

- A *static address* is fixed on your router and does not change.

- A *dynamic address* on your router changes on a regular basis.

Nowadays, most Internet access providers use dynamic IP addressing schemes. To avoid regularly changing the IP address used to remotely access your IP camera, consideration should be given to setting up a service called DDNS. Once configured, DDNS allows you to assign a domain name to your IP camera, which is always discoverable even if your router uses dynamic IP addresses.

Now that you have proven that your camera is contactable over the Internet, you need to update your HA controller to include details of your new IP camera.

HA 2.0 Access Control & Locking Systems

Secure and effective locks are absolutely essential in today's world; particularly in these recession times! In addition to automating your lights, alarm, entertainment, heating and blinds, why not set your home apart by installing some type of access control system that you could used to determine the following:

- Who is allowed to enter or exit your home?
- Which doors they can use to enter or exit your home?
- What time of the day or night family members are allowed entry and exit?

In summary, with HA 2.0 access control systems, if you have correct credentials then access in and out is a seamless process.

How a HA 2.0 Access Control System Works

The addition of access control to your HA 2.0 system can heighten security levels and provide an extra layer of convenience.

The major components of a typical HA 2.0 access control system are illustrated in Figure 3.6 and explained in the following paragraphs.

❑ **Figure 3.6 HA 2.0 Access Control Architecture**

Access control cards – Stores the 'who where and when' access control information. Popular form factors include plastic fob and cards.

A card reader at each door – This piece of hardware reads the configuration data from control cards and sends back to the home automation controller. When presented with a valid card, the reader can initiate the following actions:

- Open the door ☺
- Arm or disarm your alarm system.
- Activate various home automation scenes

A remotely controllable electronic lock – As the name implies this unit secures your door. It requires power, typically 12 or 24 volts.

A cable that runs from the card reader back to your automation controller – As illustrated a cable (I normally use Cat5) is run between the automation controller and the access reader. Two of the wires are used to carry power and two more are used for the purpose of carrying control data. The other 4 wires are spare.

Once the above items are installed correctly and configured, a HA 2.0 door and access control system allows you to do the following:

- Check the status of your door locks from your smartphone; great peace of mind feature!
- Monitor and control your door locks from anywhere with an Internet-enabled device.
- Remotely allow access to your home or holiday home for local tradesmen.
- Lock your doors automatically based on factors such as time of day and occupancy status.
- Receive notifications on your phone when the kids arrive home from school.
- In the event of an emergency (a fire for instance), your access control system can automatically open all doors.

In addition to all the serious elements of access control listed, there are also a couple of fun and enjoyable elements to installing access control readers on your front and back doors:

 No more need to fumble around for your keys – swiping a card is easy!

Secondly, you can configure these systems to trigger different scenes. Once installed, why not configure your system to turn on your favorite Internet radio station, when you swipe your card coming home from work.

Add Water & Freeze Detection

The establishment of a water alarm system involves the installation of a flood sensor. Once water flooding is detected an alert is sent straight back to your home automation controller. Water can originate from a number of sources ranging from leaking pipes to refrigerators.

Similar to the smoke alarm system, once the water sensor detects problems, your home controller will emit a loud sound and notifications are sent onwards via email, SMS and telephone calls.

Here are the steps associated with installing a flood detection sensor and interfacing with your HA 2.0 controller.

① For a start your Z-Wave alarm flood detector needs to be physically installed. These units typically comprise of two parts – a sensor located on the floor and a transceiver, which is placed high up on the wall to maximize signal strength. Note that both parts are interconnected via a cable.

② The next step is to put your controller into Include mode.

③ Undo and remove the screw from the bottom edge of the transceiver. Remove the back cover and fit appropriate batteries.

 The next step is to press the link key three times within a short period (i.e. 1 to 2 seconds).

> **! Quick Side Note from • Gerard:**
>
> Consider purchasing a wireless water valve and also interface with your HA 2.0 system. The purpose of this piece of hardware is to stop the flow of water once the leak is detected by your Z-Wave alarm flood sensor.

The icon for the flood detector will appear on your controller's interface.

 Next step is to enter a desired name for the flood detector.

 Click Save to save all settings for this device.

Freeze alarm sensors are also available that will work with your existing Z-Wave enabled system and send out alerts if freezing conditions are detected. This will improve your peace of mind and help to protect against burst pipes during periods of extreme cold. Please note that combined water and freeze detectors are available for purchase.

Practical Usage Examples

A HA 2.0 system can be customized to meet your daily living needs. The following examples describe how some of our customers are using HA 2.0 products to solve particular problems and enhance their living.

Implementation Example 1 – Enhancing Security Levels of an Elderly Couple in the UK

Requirement

An elderly couple in Birmingham, UK connected with us earlier this year and outlined that they wanted to upgrade their existing HA 2.0 system to automatically switch three lights on in the house when motion is detected in their back garden. Here is the solution that was used:

The Solution

 Their local electrician installed standard outside lights that includes motion detection functionality, which triggers locally once an intruder starts to move closer to the main house.

 These mains powered sensor lights are pretty standard and in reality do very little to deter a thief from entering the premises, so I suggested that they add an outdoor Z-wave motion sensor in the desired location. In this case as illustrated in Figure 3.7 the sensor is mounted to an outside wall on the extension.

❏ **Figure 3.7 Implementation Example 1**

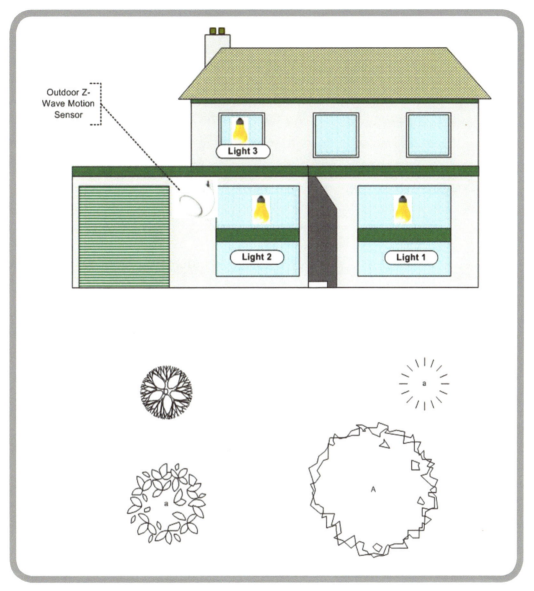

③ The electrician included the new sensor in the elderly couples existing in-home Z-Wave HA 2.0 network.

④ A scene was setup to turn on three internal lighting circuits for a period of 10 minutes once the outdoor motion sensor detects an intruder on the couple's property.

Please note that this scene can also be expanded in the future by editing the configuration to set off more lights, turn on a siren, play music or even activate a camera!

The elderly couple now have added another measure that will hopefully act as a deterrent for anybody considering a break-in to their property.

Implementation Example 2 – Create the 'Lived In' Look

Requirement

We had another homeowner (Owen based in West Cork) who uses standard light timers over the years to make his house look like it was lived in, whilst away on holidays. With the recession and increase in crime rates, Owen asked for some advice on how to transfer this functionality over to an automation system. Here is the solution that was used:

Solution

A simplified graphical view of the solution used by Owen is illustrated Figure 3.8 and explained in the following steps:

❏ Figure 3.8 Implementation Example 2

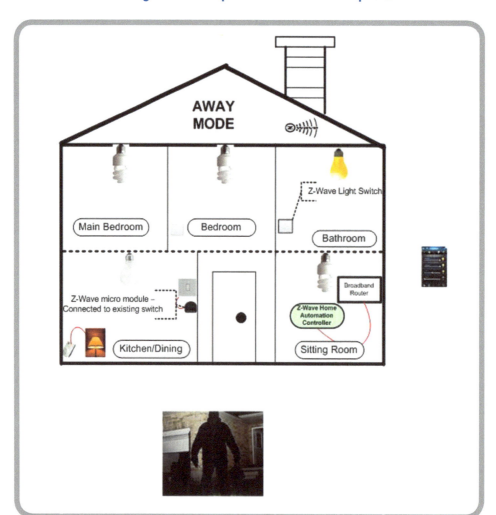

Owen got his electrical contractor to install some wireless light dimmers, switches and plug-ins around the house.

He purchased a HA 2.0 controller online and configured a scene called 'Lived In' to turn lights on and off in particular rooms at random times during the evening time – giving the illusion that there is a family member at home.

When Owen and his family are away for any extended period of time he activates the 'Lived In' scene when leaving the house, making the house look as if it is occupied.

It is hard to say for definite whether the above solution deters would-be thieves from monitoring his house. However, from speaking to him in person, the above solution has certainly enhanced his peace of mind when he is out of the house.

Implementation Example 3 – Receive a Text Message and E-mail When a Water Leak is Detected

Requirement

Our third example of how people are using HA 2.0 systems to solve specific problems involves a rack of expensive AV equipment located in a utility room! Basically, a family in Northern France, installed a sophisticated Home Automation system in their home in 2011. Everything works perfectly fine, however the centralized rack that houses their music server, structured wiring modules, home cinema receiver and multi-room amplifier is in close proximity to their washing machine. In their email to me, they outlined concerns with regards to the risk of the washing machine leaking and causing thousands of Euro worth of damage to the equipment stored in the rack.

Here is the solution that was used:

The Solution

A simplified block diagram depicting how this problem was resolved is illustrated in Figure 3.9 and explained in the steps below:

❑ **Figure 3.9 Implementation Example Water Flooding**

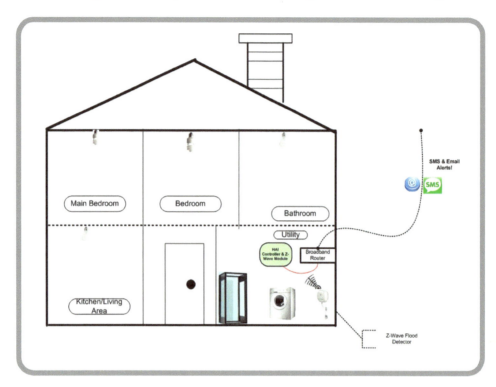

① The homeowner purchased and mounted a Z-Wave water sensor to the wall in the utility room.

② The homeowners had installed a wired based home automation during construction. In order to interconnect the Z-Wave sensor to the main controller a gateway module was used to pass alerts to the controller.

③ The automation controller was programmed to send email and SMS messages once the water detector is triggered.

④ An App now informs them immediately if their washing machine springs a leak.

These are just three simple and yet practical real life examples of how HA 2.0 systems are helping to enhance people's security and safety levels in their homes all over the world!

Things to Remember

In this chapter, here are the key take away points to remember:

● HA 2.0 systems can be pre-programmed to allow you to remotely monitor, arm and disarm your alarm using a smartphone, PC or tablet device.

- If the HA 2.0 alarm is set off, you will be automatically informed by e-mail, text or indeed phone of a break-in.

- The installation of smoke alarms increases your families' safety levels by providing you with an early warning of fire.

- IP cameras allow you to view live video images on your smartphone. Additionally, they can be configured to record live video when an alarm is detected.

- Access Control offers a secure, convenient, flexible and cost effective way of controlling who has access to your home and when that access is allowed.

- Once integrated onto your HA 2.0 network, water and freeze sensors can send you warning alerts.

Ok, that's it for now! As you see, you certainly don't have to spend much money to set up with the basic things to get started with this.

Okay, let's move onwards to the next Chapter about controlling your lights with a smartphone or tablet!

CHAPTER 4

STEP 2: ADD LIGHTING CONTROL TO YOUR HA 2.0 SYSTEM

Lighting Control Introduction

Lighting control is projected to be an extremely fast growing sector over the next five to ten years. In fact, according to a recent builder technology market study conducted by the Consumer Electronics Association, lighting control represents the second biggest increase of any home technology subsystem, eclipsing home theatre, multi-room audio and structured wiring!

Lighting control takes many forms but most fall into two categories—local and whole house control. The light switch, for instance, is a type of local lighting control. An occupancy sensor detecting motion in a room is another example. Additionally, most of us are familiar with dusk or daylight sensors and lighting timers.

The whole house approach is when lighting for the entire home is managed by a central light control panel system. These systems can be designed to manage lighting for different times of the day, special events or occasional occurrences. Often, automated lighting control devices are integrated with other security systems, IP cameras and motorized blinds control.

Here are some of the things you can do with a lighting control system:

- Control virtually any light fixture, outside light or lamp in your home.

- Monitor & control your home's lighting from your iPhone, iPad or Android device.

- Turn lights automatically ON at sunset and OFF at sunrise.

- Turn lights ON when a room is occupied and OFF when it's unoccupied.

- Use motion sensors to simulate a presence in the house when away on holiday.

- Set the lights to dim when watching a movie or TV channel.

- Adjust the dim levels of particular lights based on outside brightness levels.

- In the event of a fire, all lights are turned on to assist in evacuating the house.

Main Benefits of Automating my Lights

There are three headline benefits associated with automating your lights: energy savings, improved security levels and improved ambience.

 Lighting Control Saves You Energy

Over the past number of years, awareness of how green technologies such as light control systems can reduce a homeowners energy consumption levels has increased dramatically. Not only can the benefits of a whole house lighting system be seen but the effects can be felt in the wallet as well. According to recent research reports, lighting accounts for 10 to 15% of our household electrical bills. Unfortunately, 50% of this energy is wasted by inefficient lighting sources or careless consumers. With the steady rise in energy costs, most homeowners would agree that it's fiscally savvy and environmentally responsible to deliver the correct amount of light when and where it is actually required. The ability to use a lighting control system to minimize the environmental impact of residential units is seen by many as one of the primary reasons why demand for lighting control solutions has surged in recent times. Here are some specifics with regards to the energy saving argument associated with lighting control systems:

 Dimming lights reduces overhead costs and slows the rate that light bulbs deteriorate. Most houses around the world use standard ON/OFF light switches. So no matter what the light levels are in a room, when a switch is toggled on, the light bulb is drawing the maximum amount of power and operating at 100%. Replacing ON/OFF switches with dimmers means that you can adjust the levels to the desired level of lighting. For instance most light loads can be dimmed to approximately 70% before people will even notice the difference. This not only cuts down on the cost of using the light bulb but also helps to create the right atmosphere in a room if included as part of an automation scene. Additionally the soft ramping up feature of lighting control systems helps to extend the bulb life even further! Further statistics on the affect that dimming has on energy savings and incandescent bulb life is described in Table 4.1.

❑ **Table 4.1 – Effect of Dimming on Electricity and Incandescent Light Bulbs**

Lights dimmed this much	Electrical Savings	Extends Bulb Life
10%	10%	2X
25%	20%	4X
50%	40%	20X
75%	60%	>20X

- *Scheduling* allows you to automatically turn ON and OFF lights at particular times of the day. Such capabilities can be optimized to reduce energy consumption levels at home.

- *Sensors* can be used in conjunction with a lighting control system to ensure lights only come on when a room is occupied or when natural light levels are too low to see properly.

- *Ease of use:* Rather than wiring a bank of switches on the wall to control multiple lights (typical of a traditional lighting system in a restaurant); you can setup a single button on both the wall and within your lighting control app to control multiple lights – all at once.

② **Lighting Control Improves Security & Safety Levels**

Perhaps the greatest lifestyle benefits of a lighting control system are the safety and security features. The types of security features provided by many of the modern lighting control systems can include:

- Keyless remote lighting control fobs that are programmed to turn ON one or all of the house lights, open the garage door, and even deactivate the security system during the arrival of the homeowner.

- Lighting scenes can be programmed to turn lights ON and OFF randomly when people are away on holidays, discouraging potential thieves from entering the premises.

- Lighting control systems can also potentially be integrated with other security systems incorporated into the housing structure.

Lighting Control Improves Convenience & Ambience Levels

This is more of a 'soft' non-measurable benefit that is inextricably linked to lighting control systems – higher ambience and comfort levels. Scenes that allow you to set pre-determined lighting levels for multiple light fixtures in a room, or in fact all over the house, is one of the key features of lighting control systems that people use to make life more convenient. In addition to utilizing scenes, lighting control can also help to add an element of ambience to your home. For instance, when our family sits down in the evening to eat, I tap a button on our iPad, and instanteously create an atmosphere by dimming the kitchen and dining room lights to 60% intensity levels.

In addition to the above three benefits, light switches used by lighting control systems typically look nicer and helps to improve the aesthetics of your walls.

Lighting Control System Options

Your options for installing a lighting control system fall into two broad categories: wired and wireless.

Both of these approaches are discussed in the following subsections.

Wired Lighting Control

If you are building a new house or involved in some renovations and the budget permits you to install a lighting control system then you should definitely consider running some physical cable.

As illustrated in Figure 4.1 a typical wired based lighting control system consists of four main components:

❑ **Figure 4.1 Architecture of Wired Lighting Control System**

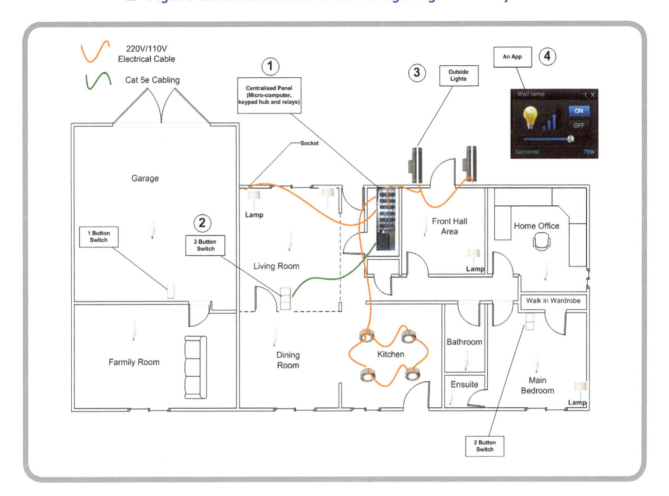

The *centralized panel* normally consists of three hardware modules:

- An intelligent micro-computer – acts as the brains of your system.

- A central control unit which communicates with a hub device that acts as a termination point for the low voltage Cat 5e cables that run from a centralized lighting controller panel in your house to each of the lighting switches connected to the home lighting system.

- High voltage dimming relays which are connected to various types of lighting loads using electrical power cable. These relays are also able to control non-dimmable loads such as compact fluorescent lighting fixtures and appliances.

The *lighting keypads* installed at any desired location in the home or business transmit ON, OFF and Dim commands over the Cat5 cable to the centralized control panel. Each keypad can accommodate a number of buttons, any one of which may operate a load or scene. Lighting keypads are available in different guises and styles to suit the décor of your rooms. Most lighting control manufacturers also provide an engraving service that allows you to identify and personalize your light switches.

Various types of *light loads* ranging from incandescent bulbs and electronic low-voltage transformers for in-ceiling spots to fluorescent and LED light fittings.

In addition to using a wall light switch (keypad), most lighting control systems also come with an *App* that allows you to switch lights and scenes ON and OFF. In addition to standard functions, these Apps also allow you to dim and set off different lighting scenes.

How to Install a Wired based Whole House Lighting Control System?

Installing a properly planned wired home lighting control system can be done with remarkably little effort. An introduction to the steps associated with planning and installing a wired based lighting control system is briefly outlined below:

STEP 1   Planning

Wired lighting systems are usually planned and designed during the development of architectural drawings for the home. The planning for the location of various light fixtures such as in-ceiling lights and switched-wall outlets for portable lamps are all essential for proper light distribution in a home. The number of lighting circuits will depend on the size of the home in square feet and the number of family members.

You need to spend the necessary planning time up front to be sure that the system is perfectly tailored to your needs. For instance, the lighting atmosphere will be different in each of the rooms. Table 4.2 provides some guidelines for creating different types of lighting atmospheres in various rooms.

❑ **Table 4.2 – Differing in-room lighting atmospheres:**

Room	Suggestions
Living and Sitting Rooms	These rooms are normally used for relaxation and entertainment purposes, thus the lighting selected for these areas needs to create a cozy atmosphere for your family. Multiple circuits, wall lights and extensive use of dimming technologies are often used to achieve the desired effect.
Kitchen	The kitchen is used for practical functions such as preparing and cooking food. Bright down-lighters are more appropriate for this part of the house.
Bathroom	Low voltage waterproof lighting and sensors are often used in bathrooms to improve family safety levels.
Home Office	Working long hours on a PC requires a constant level of lighting. Whichever room you plan to use as a home office, consideration should be given to installing a sensor that measures light levels and interfaces with your HA 2.0 controller to keep a constant light level in the home office.
Outside	Outside lights are used to create a perception of safety and style. Interfacing with a HA 2.0 controller can help to achieve this desired effect.

STEP 2   Get your Electrical Contractor to Rough-In the Necessary Wiring

The incorporation of a wired light control system into a new house or apartment requires the use of low voltage Cat 5e cables that run from the centralized lighting controller panel in your house to each of the lighting switches connected to the home lighting system. Rough-in consists of the following tasks, which are primarily done by your electrical contractor:

Task 1: Install the centralized lighting control panel

The centralized panel is mounted in an air-conditioned space near the main electrical breaker box. A normal location would be inside a closet or utility room. The location of your panel would need to be accessible as you will be connecting to the panel at a later date with your PC to do some configuration. Also be sure to check local electrical codes for compliance, when mounting your control panel.

Task 2: Identify physical locations for your light switches

You now need to walk through from room to room with your electrical contractor and mark up locations where lighting control switches and dimmers are to be installed.

Tip: Be sure to put a switch location on either side of the master bed at a position slightly higher than the top of the bed so that you can control some load and scene switches from either side of the master bed.

Task 3: Pull the Wire

When the time is right during the construction phase, your electrical contractor will use a lighting control design document, as a basis for running both high voltage and Cat5e cable back to the centralized panel.

Task 4: Protect equipment from dust damage

Get your electrician to seal up the centralized panel duct tape, masking tape, or other materials so that all wire and labels will be protected from any construction damage.

STEP 3   Second Fix & Complete Physical Installation

When all the sheet rock (aka slabbing here in Europe), painting, and finish work has been completed, you are ready to terminate all lighting loads, keypads and low voltage wiring.

Task 1: Complete High-Voltage Connections

All 220V or 110V connections must be made and tested at the lighting control panel by your licensed electrician.

Task 2: Keypad Installation

Install each lighting control keypad at the proper location. This will involve:

- Crimping RJ-45 connectors on both ends of the Cat5e cables
- Testing connectivity
- Physically installing and attaching to the backbox.

STEP 4   Programming & Configuration

Program the system using a PC, laptop or even a tablet! A screenshot of the software used to configure a wired lighting control system is shown in Figure 4.2.

❑ **Figure 4.2 Sample Lighting Control Software Configuration System**

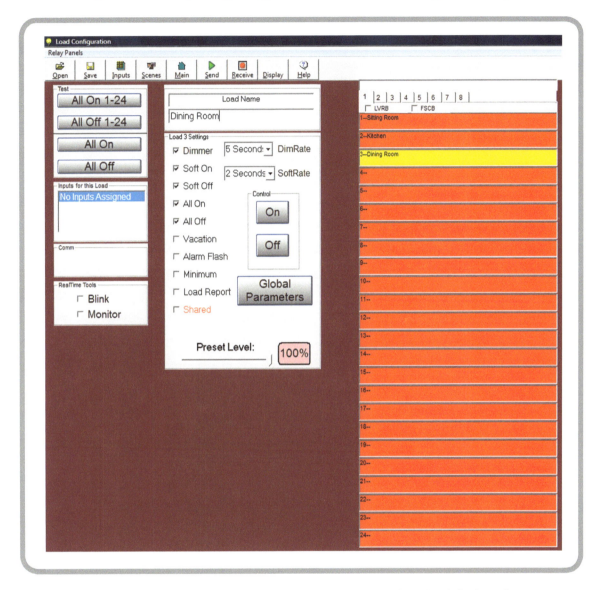

The manual accompanying your system will provide a more detailed insight into how to correctly configure your new system.

Wireless Lighting Control Systems

For houses that are already built and do not have the necessary cables pre-installed, homeowners generally opt for an easy-to-install and affordable wireless lighting control solution.

As illustrated in Figure 4.3, HA 2.0 wireless lighting systems typically comprise of a number of smart pluggable devices, wall switches or dimmers and micro-switches that use radio frequencies to communicate with each other and back to a centralized home automation controller.

❑ Figure 4.3 Floor Plan Layout Z-Wave Lighting Control

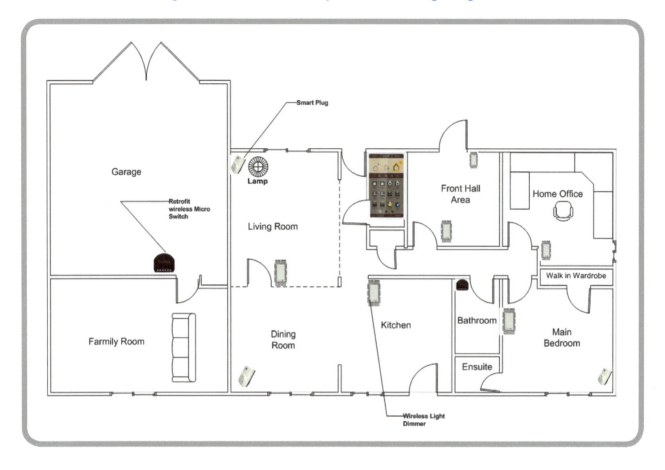

Wireless systems based on protocols such as Zigbee, INSTEON and Z-Wave require no new cabling yet offer many of the benefits of a hardwired system

How to Install an End-to-End Wireless Lighting Control System

In terms of installation, it is relatively easy to start building out a wireless lighting control system, and involves the following steps:

Select the lighting devices in your home that you want to control.

Purchase some pluggable wireless light modules.

Configure your modules to 'talk' with your home automation controller. A basic reference architecture of the communication path between your App and the light bulb is illustrated in Figure 4.4.

❑ **Figure 4.4 Basic Reference Example - Zwave Wireless Lighting**

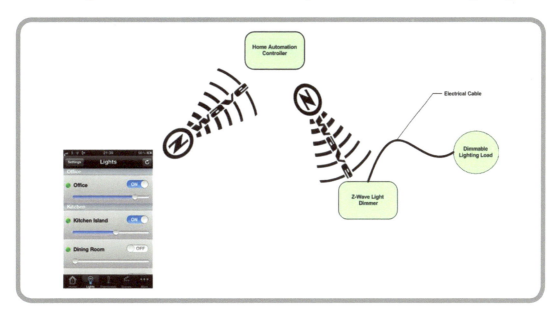

That's it! You can now control your in-home lighting via a smart phone or tablet device over the Internet.

Over time, you can start adding more lamp modules and if you decide to get adventurous, why not start to automate some of your existing wall mounted light switches.

There are two distinct approaches to incorporating existing lighting switches into your in-home automation system:

Warning: If you are not knowledgeable and skilled in working with electricity, do not execute the steps below. Instead, issue the steps outlined below to a certified electrician or someone who posses the correct skills.

Replacing the existing light switch –
Typical retrofit steps for this approach involve:

- Turn OFF the local electrical power feeding the switch location and verify that there is no power present using a voltage meter or test light.

- Remove the existing switch. Note which wires are the Earth, Live, Neutral and Switch Wire. Please note that in older homes, particularly in UK and Ireland, there will only exist an Earth, a Live and a Switched Live. Also the colours of the wires can vary from the standard – particularly for older properties.

- Connect your wireless lighting control dimmer or switch to the appropriate cables.

- Test and re-fit switch or dimmer back onto the wall.

Register new switch on your automation controller.

Retaining the existing light switch and adding a micro-switch module – the steps involved with installing a micro-switch are more or less the same as completely replacing the light switch. There are one or two extra steps that need to be taken and are outlined in our video course.

Which to Choose: Wired or Wireless Lighting Control?

Table 4.3 explains the characteristics of each approach.

> ❗**Quick Side Note from Gerard:**
>
> It would be more prudent to turn off the main electricity feed into your home, before you continue.

❏ **Table 4.3 – Comparison of Wired and Wireless Lighting Control Characteristics**

	Type of construction	Costs	Reliability	Features
Wired lighting control systems	New build	Can be expensive – depends on the number of circuits to be automated.	High levels of reliability are one of the key advantages of wired lighting control systems.	Wired systems will typically support more functionality compared to their wireless counterparts.
Wireless lighting control system	Primarily retrofit and is ideal if you don't want the disruption of running new cables throughout your home.	Generally less expensive when compared to larger Cat5e based systems.	Materials included in the fabric of your home such as concrete, plaster, and metal can cause problems for a wireless system.	In an effort to keep manufacturing costs low, some wireless lighting control systems have cut back on certain advanced functionalities.

As you can see from the table above, wired lighting controls are preferable if you are building a new home. They are typically more expensive but have advantages over wireless systems in terms of functionality and reliability. Wireless is great if you have a limited budget and you want to start small and grow the number of automated switches over time. When going down the wireless route, you need to be cognizant of potential issues such as range and interference. As wireless technologies mature these issues are becoming less significant.

Lighting Control as a Mainstream Product

The features and advantages of modern lighting control systems are truly incredible. Technological advancements have given us comprehensive and affordable home lighting controls that can do things Thomas Edison would have never dreamed were possible. And more and more people are realizing and taking advantage of these benefits. Affordability and convincing homeowners that automating home lighting systems is an essential purchase, especially compared to the more obvious home control categories like home theatre and whole house music, are the main challenges for those who want to see the mainstream proliferation of lighting control systems.

Practical Usage Examples

A lighting control system is highly customizable. Here are four examples of how our own family use lighting control:

Implementation Example 1 – Use an App to Activate a Lighting Scene at Dinner Time

Requirement

One of the things I wanted to do with our lighting control system was to be able to tap a button on my iPhone and dim the main dining room centre light level to 75% and simultaneously turn on a side lamp. This scene then would be activated most evenings when the family is sitting down to eat dinner.

The Solution

The items of equipment used are illustrated in Figure 4.5 and setup is explained in the following steps:

❏ **Figure 4.5 Dinner time Scene**

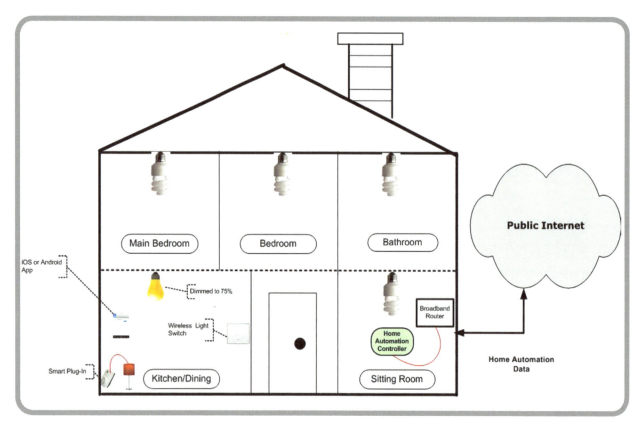

①   To control the overhead light a wall dimmer equipped with wireless technology was installed and setup.

TIP: If you prefer to keep an existing light switch, then it's also possible to install a small wireless micro-switch that fits into the back box.

②   To control the lamp in the dining area, an inexpensive wireless smart plug-in module was configured.

③   Both wireless modules were setup on my existing HA 2.0 controller

④   I setup a scene on the controller called 'Dining Time'.

⑤   This scene gets activated via my iPhone app pretty regularly in our house and works really well!

Implementation Example 2 – Set-up Motion Activated Lighting Control in the Main Bathroom

Requirement

Olive and I are always 'giving out' to our three older kids to turn off the lights when they leave a room. This has met with limited success over the years! For some reason this minor, but slightly annoying issue of leaving the light and ceiling fan on is most prominent in the main bathroom. One of my little DIY projects over the Christmas holiday period last year was to add the following automated functions to the bathroom:

- Automatically turn on the light and fan when any family members go into the bathroom.

- Turn the light and fan off again 30 seconds after they leave.

The Solution

The items of equipment used are illustrated in Figure 4.6 and setup is explained in the following steps:

❏ **Figure 4.6 Motion Activated Lighting Control in the Main Bathroom**

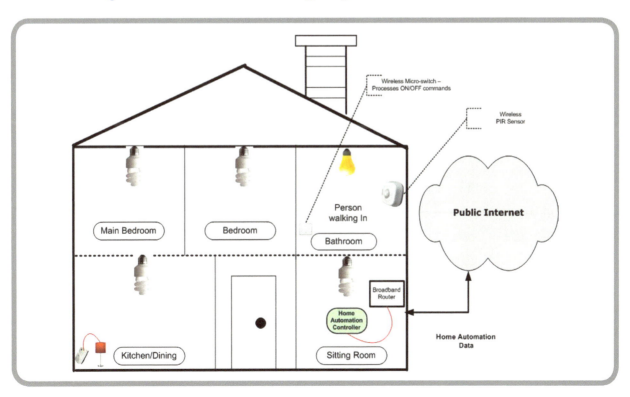

① A Passive InfraRed (PIR) Motion sensor, in this case was installed on the bathroom wall.

② Rather than changing my existing light switch, a small wireless micro-switch got installed inside the backbox of the light switch.

③ I programmed both the PIR and micro-switch on my existing HA 2.0 controller to do the following:

- When the PIR senses motion, it automatically communicates wirelessly with the HA 2.0 controller.

- The HA 2.0 controller is then configured to issue an ON command to the micro-switch, which in turn powers the light fixture and the fan.

- Once motion is undetected for a configurable period of time (In our case we choose 30 seconds), the controller subsequently sends an OFF command to the wireless switch to stop passing current to the bathroom light and the fan.

The benefits (although small when you compare to what's going on in the world) include:

- A reduction in the amount of electricity used when the bathroom is unoccupied, to eliminating the hassle of feeling around for a switch in the dark.

- We are giving out less to less reminders to the kids now ☺

Implementation Example 3 – Control all the Lights in the House from an App

Requirement

Rather than going into each room at night before heading to bed, I like the idea of tapping a single ALL OFF icon on my smartphone HA 2.0 App before going to sleep. As such, I set up an ALL OFF scene on my existing HA Controller earlier in the year.

The Solution

Figure 4.7 shows the components that I use, and a brief overview of what actions need to be executed are outlined in the following four steps:

❏ **Figure 4.7 Control all the lights in the house from an App**

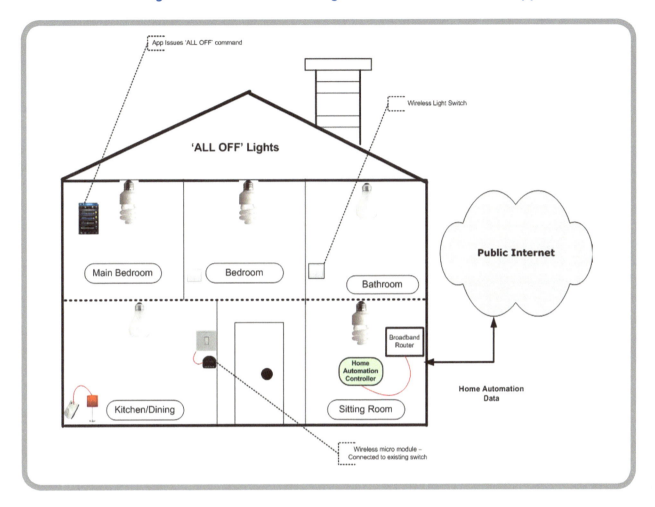

① Before going ahead and setting up this function, make sure that you have added either wireless or wired control functionality to each of your lighting circuits. Use a certified electrician if you are not comfortable working with high voltage circuits – which is the case for most people. In my case, all of my lighting circuits were controllable.

② Setup was simple and only involved configuring an ALL OFF scene called "Goodnight" on my HA 2.0 controller.

③ I also configured an 'ALL ON' scene, which as the name implies turns on every light on the house instantly. It's more of a safety feature that I could use if something serious happened in the middle of the night. 'Touch wood' this scene never gets activated.

④ So at night, I am typically the last family member into bed, I tap the "Goodnight" icon within my App and every light in the house gets switched off! Now that's what I call lazy ☺

Implementation Example 4 – Dark House in Evening

Requirement

Olive hates coming back to a dark house – particularly in windy and cold winter evenings here in Ireland. I was given the task of coming up with a solution!

Solution

Pretty easy to do:

① I got a local handyman who helps me out from time to time to replace the existing switch used to control the porch light with a wireless ON/OFF switch.

② As with all new wireless products, I included the new switch in the in-home wireless network.

③ I created a scene called 'Arriving home', which turns on the outside porch light automatically at sunset during the winter months.

④ It works a treat!

Things to Remember

Inside this chapter you learned about both wired and wireless lighting control systems – here are the key take home points to remember:

● Lighting control enhances the enjoyment and value of your home, adds security for peace of mind, and contributes to savings on your electricity bill.

● Lighting control can be used as a mechanism to deter crime at your home and provides you with the ability to use a smartphone, PC browser or tablet to control the lights in your home.

● Hardwired lighting control systems are suitable for extensions and new builds.

● If you are like most of us and did not run Cat5 cable to your light switches, then affordable Z-Wave, Zigbee or INSTEON light switches, dimmers and plug-in outlets are the solution.

- Many of the wireless lighting control systems are designed for at-home do-it-yourselfers; so are pretty easy to setup and configure.

- If you do not have enough electrical skills, hire an electrician for a couple of hours to install your wireless micro-switches and HA 2.0 enabled switches and dimmers.

You now need to take action in the form of purchasing the correct hardware items, retrofitting and adding to your existing HA 2.0 controller.

Okay, let's get stuck into the next chapter!

CHAPTER 5

STEP 3: ADD HEATING & SMART ENERGY CONTROL TO YOUR HA 2.0 SYSTEM

There is a perception that the initial euphoria surrounding smart home energy management has started to wear off. According to recent surveys, however, it appears that people still remain concerned about their monthly electricity bill – and in fact people are strongly interested in monitoring and managing their energy usage.

Using a HA 2.0 system to monitor and control energy usage is one approach that people can implement to save money on their electricity bills.

Once energy management is implemented and interfaced correctly with a HA 2.0 system, you will be able to:

- Remotely record the amount of electricity each appliance and electronic device is using and schedule them to turn ON and OFF as required.

- Rather than wait for your monthly electricity bill you will be able to visualize energy consumption and CO_2 emission levels in real time.

- Receive energy usage alerts by email or SMS text.

- Automatically control lighting and appliances based on energy use and occupancy.

- Monitor your home's energy use and cost from anywhere with your smartphone or tablet.

Unfortunately, for a number of reasons the uptake amongst the general population of energy management products and services has been slow. The hope in this chapter is that you enable and use your new automation system to at least monitor the energy used every month and make some minor tweaks here and there to reduce your electricity bill.

One of the reasons we use and waste so much energy in our homes is that we do not have the tools to see or control our energy use. Home automation is key for energy management – in fact the two can't really be separated. It not only acts as a platform whereby consumers can control various systems in their home, but also enables people see where energy wastage is occurring 'under their noses'!

Adding Energy Management to your HA 2.0 System

> **❝** *Home automation is seen by a few (including myself) as a key mechanism of identifying wastage and encouraging homeowners to make their homes more energy efficient.* **❞**

Energy is wasted by people because it is invisible and most of us don't analyze and monitor. Home automation is seen by a few (including myself) as a key mechanism of identifying wastage and encouraging homeowners to make their homes more energy efficient.

Adding energy monitoring and management capabilities to your home automation system, typically involves the installation of a variety of devices. Energy saving devices fall primarily into three broad categories:

1. Those Used to Reduce your Energy Wasted by Lighting & Appliances

The role of devices used in conjunction with your HA 2.0 controller to cut down on energy wastage by lights and kitchen appliances are described in the following Table 5.1.

❑ **Table 5.1 HA 2.0 Energy Saving Devices**

Energy management device	Description
Smart Appliance Switches	Most people do not fully realize that electricity costs fluctuate depending on the time of day. In other words, it is cheaper to run your washing machine off peak during the middle of the day. Devices such as smart appliance switches can allow you to realize cost savings by automatically turning certain kitchen appliances on at times of the day where electricity costs are at their lowest. In addition to scheduling ON and OFF periods, these units can also report kWh energy usage of devices such as lamps and home entertainment equipment and appliances that have high energy requirements back to your HA 2.0 controller when requested. These modules are also controllable via an App, allowing you to ensure optimal efficiency. Installation is simple, you just plug your kitchen appliance, lamp or whatever into the switch, which in turn gets plugged into the mains socket on the wall.
Smart Lamp Switch Modules	These modules allow you to turn connected pluggable lamps ON and OFF remotely so you can control electric usage.
Motion sensors	Motion sensors can be used to control lights or indeed a group of lights. These units can be programmed to detect the presence of people in a room and turn OFF lights and ceiling fans when the room becomes unoccupied.
Wireless Light switch Modules	These units allow you to control your lights locally using a standard switch, or remotely with an App.

2. Those Used to Reduce Costs of Home Heating

According to industry analysts, heating our homes can account for between 40% and 50% of our electricity; this percentage is higher if you live in a warm country, as you also require cooling functionality.

In view of the emphasis nowadays on energy conservation in households around the world, consideration should be given to adding control of the boiler (heating system) to your HA 2.0 smartphone or tablet App – doing so provides the following benefits:

The system will be able to turn off automatically both the heating and the hot water when you leave the house.

It also lets you turn on the heating and the hot water before you get home via your smartphone to create a comfortable climate, when arriving home from work in the evening.

Moreover, special conditional statements can be programmed to control temperature and help in saving energy. Here are a couple of examples :

 While you are away on holidays the system can automatically switch off the heating and hot water to save energy.

 Whilst at work you can schedule the heating system to stay off until a family member arrives back home – for instance you might want to raise the temperature levels from 18°C to maybe 20°C when a presence sensor in the hall detects that the kids have arrived home from school.

HA 2.0 heating control systems enable you to set different temperature levels for each room in your house and set up a weekly heating schedule that matches your lifestyle.

The types of components used to build an automated heating control system include:

- Smart thermostats
- Wireless TRV's
- Temperature sensors

Smart Thermostats

❝ *Before deciding on purchasing a new Wi-Fi smart thermostat it's important that you check the wiring behind your existing thermostat.* ❞

A smart thermostat, typically wall mounted, measures the ambient temperature in the room using a temperature sensor in the device itself. Once you define a comfort temperature in the room the thermostat will try to achieve this reading by opening and closing boiler valves, also called actuators.

Additionally, smart thermostats also provide heat scheduling functionality. A heating schedule defines deviations from the comfort temperature. Depending on the model of your smart thermostat, these devices can accept and execute multiple temperature changes over a particular time period – i.e. day, week or month.

Smart thermostats are both controllable locally and remotely via a smartphone, PC or tablet device.

There are four types of smart thermostats to choose from:

Wired thermostats: As the name implies, physical cable is required between the thermostat and the controller or actuator that switches your boiler ON and OFF.

Z-Wave thermostats: They operate on the same principle as wired thermostats, except that they communicate with the boiler via radio frequency. In Europe, particularly, the wireless Z-Wave based smart thermostats are nowhere near polished enough for the mainstream population to set up and configure! However Z-Wave thermostats in the US and other parts of the world are quite popular and readily available at a number of online stores.

Zigbee Tthermostats: With regards to Zigbee, many of the utility companies around the world are using the protocol in their smart meters. As a result of demand from the utility industry, product manufacturers are designing digital thermostats that include Zigbee wireless communication capabilities. Once installed and interfaced with a smart meter Zigbee thermostats provide the following types of information:

- Current cost of energy

- How much energy you have used

- How much your utility bill will be this month

The availability of this information helps you control energy consumption and related costs. As of writing, Zigbee thermostats are only sold to utility companies and specialized installers.

Wi-Fi thermostat controls: These thermostats are hardwired to a boiler and included in your in-home Wi-Fi network. You do need to understand a little bit about IP address configuration and consideration should be given to using a qualified electrician or heating professional to do the hard wiring stuff. Before deciding on purchasing a new Wi-Fi smart thermostat it's important that you check the wiring behind your existing thermostat. If you have three wires, excluding the earth, then you can upgrade. If not, then you may have issues with regards to installation. You'll obviously need a router (includes port forwarding capabilities) to provide connectivity to the Internet and an App to control your thermostat from anywhere in the world.

How you install your smart thermostat will depend on the make and model – here are some guidelines however:

① An interface module that connects to your boiler equipment is installed first.

② The smart thermostat is mounted on a wall approximately 1.5 metres (4 to 5 feet) above the floor in a prominent location in your house – the main sitting room area for instance. Please avoid the following locations:

- Close to other heat sources such as lights

- In line with direct sunlight

- In the kitchen

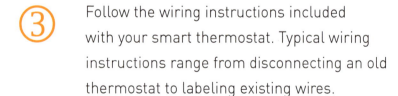

Quick Side Note from Gerard:

Smart thermostats can work in standalone mode without been connected to a HA 2.0 system.

③ Follow the wiring instructions included with your smart thermostat. Typical wiring instructions range from disconnecting an old thermostat to labeling existing wires.

④ Establish communication between the boiler interface module and the smart thermostat.

⑤ Establish communication between the smart thermostat and your HA 2.0 controller.

⑥ Once the smart thermostat and the interface module are powered up and working correctly, the smart thermostat needs to be connected to your App!

If you're comfortable with installing power outlets and terminating wires then you should be able to execute the above installation steps. Otherwise hire a trained contractor to install your smart thermostat. Here are three pragmatic tips that you might want to consider when dealing with HVAC installers:

- Communicate on a regular basis with the HVAC contractor.
- Let him know that you are supplying smart thermostats to control the heating or air conditioning systems.
- Have the manuals and wiring diagrams printed and available when discussing the installation.

Wireless TRVs

Radiator thermostats, also known as TRVs (thermostatic radiator valves) give you the opportunity to define different ambient temperatures for each room in your house – all from a smartphone or iPad! They operate by measuring room temperature, adjusting the valve, and trying to achieve a desired heating set-point. Here is how I have configured our own Z-Wave enabled TRVs around the house:

- During the weekdays (9 in the morning to 5 in the evening), TRVs keep the heat off in all the bedrooms.
- The TRVs enable heating in the evenings in the sitting room, kitchen and dining area.
- I have the TRVs configured on my iPhone to ensure that the main bathroom and bedrooms are heated to an appropriate level in the morning and just before bed.

To help you to increase energy efficiency at home, TRVs also include a heating schedule that lists deviations from the comfort temperature in rooms. Newer models of TRVs include a scheduler that allows you to set-up various different set-points for each day of a 7 day week.

TRV units are controllable at any time via a HA 2.0 App or locally using buttons.

Temperature Sensors

Temperature sensors are typically used to report alerts back to your smartphone or tablet if the temperature reaches a particular threshold limit. In addition to warning you of errant temperatures in particular rooms, this information could be used by your HA 2.0 controller to carry out a particular action – turning OFF the boiler for instance.

I have personally found that these units are particularly useful for setting up automation systems for elderly people in their homes. Sudden changes in temperature levels can cause health problems – temperature sensors may be used as a precaution to alert family members of such events.

These sensor types are also commonly found in bathrooms, greenhouses, wine cellars and garages.

3. Those used to Monitor the Energy Usage

The main purpose of home energy monitoring units is to report your home's total real-time wattage and Kwh usage back to the home automation controller.

Electricians are not typically required to install a home energy monitor as there is no specific requirement to work on exposed high voltage cable. Installation involves placing a clamp around the incoming mains supply to detect energy usage for the entire house. Once the clamp is in place, the home energy monitor needs to be paired (included) into your HA 2.0 network before it can wirelessly report electricity usage to your home automation control unit.

The interface that is used to monitor energy usage obviously varies between systems.

Using Home Automation Systems to Lower Costs

By utilizing the energy monitoring and management capabilities of your automation system not only will you be able to lower your utility bills but also help to protect the planet! It's not, however, enough to interface the home energy management sub-system with your HA 2.0 controller; you also need to take actions to ensure that you reap the rewards of investing in the various hardware items identified previously. Here are some practical usage tips:

 Regularly access the energy section of your home automation portal to see the effect of turning down power-hungry devices, unplugging unused equipment or installing power-strips that let you turn off the electricity to devices that you don't need.

 Create some energy saving scenes – here are two examples:

■ Create a scene that utilizes motion sensors to turn lights OFF when a room is vacant for more than five minutes. Particularly useful if you have a young family and you are constantly 'reminding' your kids to turn OFF the lights around the house!

- Get your HA 2.0 controller to turn off the heating in a room if someone leaves a window wide open!

③ Set the dimming levels on your wireless light switches to 75% and save up to 20 percent or more off your monthly electricity costs,

④ Setup some timed events – here are two examples:

- Set your outside lights to turn off at sunrise.

- Set your boiler to turn off at 10 p.m. each evening during the winter months.

Practical Usage Examples

The following examples describe how some of our customers are using HA 2.0 products to solve particular problems related to heating control:

Implementation Example 1 – Turn the Heating on from a Smartphone, While Commuting from Work!

Requirement

Having tighter control of their boiler systems is one of many approaches that people are using to cut home heating bills. An app combined with a home automation system allows you to interface with your boiler system on a real-time basis from anywhere in the world.

In this user case, we recently received an email enquiry from a guy in Boston with regards to using his smartphone to turn his heating system ON and OFF. Here is the text of his initial email.

Hi,

Looking for an Android app based system that allows me to turn my heating system on when I am on the way home from work.

Appreciate any guidance or product recommendations that you could provide,

Thanks,

Michael

The Solution

It turns out from a follow up Skype call that Michael lives in a house that is over 20 years old and re-wiring was not an option.

The solution that I proposed to him is graphically illustrated in Figure 5.1 and explained briefly in the following steps:

❑ **Figure 5.1 Turn the Heating ON from a smartphone whilst on the way home from work**

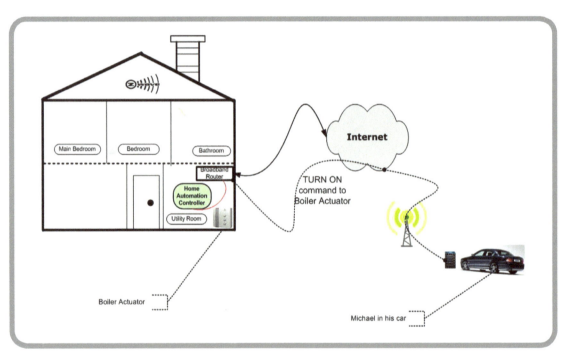

①   Purchase two wireless smart thermostats (upstairs and downstairs).

②   Contact your boiler contractor and get him or her to connect the new smart thermostats to the existing boiler equipment and confirm that everything works correctly.

③   Interface the smart thermostat with some type of HA 2.0 controller or gateway.

④   Setup and programme the smart thermostat to ensure that 'Turn ON and OFF' commands are sent from your App.

Michael went ahead with my advice and now has more flexibility in controlling his boiler to suit his lifestyle needs.

Implementation Example 2 – Commercial Installation of Wired Smart Thermostats

Requirement

A private nursing home owner approached us looking for a system that provided simple-to-use touch-screen thermostats in each of the bedrooms and also stipulated that each of the thermostats had to be accessible via a smartphone. Nursing homes for elderly people by their very nature are highly regulated; as a result a robust solution had to be designed and implemented.

The Solution

Since reliability was a key requirement, it was decided to use physical cable as a basis to build the new heating control network. The wiring infrastructure that was used in the installation is illustrated below.

❑ **Figure 5.2 Inter-connecting multiple smart thermostats with a home automation controller**

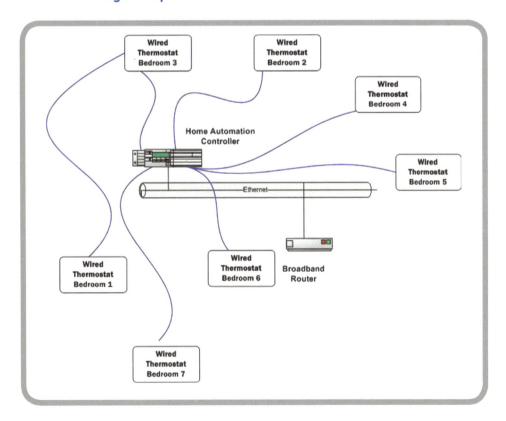

As you can see, Cat5e cable was run from each of the smart thermostats back to the home automation controller. Thus, when the nursing home owner wants to adjust the temperature in one of the resident's rooms, he simply uses his App to communicate with the HA 2.0 controller, which in turn sends an adjust temperature command over the physical cable to the thermostat.

Although the above example references a small commercial installation, the architecture outlined is also popular for new residential builds.

Things to Remember

Inside this chapter you learned about adding energy management functionality to your HA 2.0 system – here are the key take points to remember:

- Integrating your heating or indeed cooling system with a HA 2.0 controller can bring out about significant financial savings.

- With Home Automation you can control virtually any central heating or cooling system on your iPhone or Android device.

- The HA 2.0 paradigm supports a number of energy saving devices ranging from motion sensors and wireless light switches to smart thermostats and energy monitoring units.

- Once configured correctly, smart thermostats allow you to:

  - Remotely raise and lower the temperature.

  - Set up modes and schedules that match your daily lifestyle

  - Use your App to turn the heating system ON or OFF from any part of the world!

- There are four variants of smart thermostats, namely wired, Z-Wave, Zigbee and Wi-Fi enabled units. Zigbee has an advantage over the other three in the sense that the global utility industry is using Zigbee for smart grid rollouts. However Zigbee thermostats are not generally available and are normally sold directly to utility companies.

CHAPTER 6

STEP 4: ADD MULTI-ROOM MUSIC 2.0 TO YOUR HA 2.0 SYSTEM

The multi-room music (MRM) system is one of my favourite HA 2.0 features installed at our home recently. As with all of these systems it adds some cool elements to our day-to-day life including:

- The system is setup as an elegant wakeup alarm system to play the local radio station in the mornings, through the virtually invisible in-ceiling speakers in our own and the kids' bedrooms each weekday morning.

- The kids use an their smartphones to control and listen to their personal iTunes libraries and Internet radio stations in their own rooms.

- We often have the system playing in the background as we go about our evenings at home.

A MRM system refers to a home entertainment environment that sends music from a centralized location to multiple rooms. Because, the main source equipment is located centrally, the only components present in the various rooms include a set of speakers (typically located in the wall or ceiling) and possibly a wall mounted volume control.

With next generation MRM 2.0 systems, smartphones or tablets are typically used to select and control your music sources. With the older MRM systems, music sources typically consisted of a CD player, a radio tuner and a cable set-top box. MRM 2.0 systems use the following as sources:

- Internet radio channels

- iTunes and Windows based music libraries

- Online music services

Wired Multi-room Music System Options

If your house is not pre-wired for an audio system or you have no plans to break open walls and ceilings to retrofit new wiring, then it probably makes more sense to skip the following paragraphs and jump down to the section on wireless music systems.

If however you are embarking on a new construction type project, then there are three different levels of wired based house music systems to choose from and each of them have different attributes.

1. Entry level Systems

In its most basic form a multi-room music system for your home simply involves the running of standard speaker cables between a centralized amplifier, which is connected to a music source, such as a CD player, a traditional radio, a PC music server (a device that stores music on a hard disk) or an MP3 player, to different sets of speakers. The speakers can be installed in different locations throughout the house or apartment. Speaker types range from those that can be flush mounted with the surface of the building (namely in-ceiling speakers and in-wall speakers) to free standing speakers that are often found in the living or dining room.

The overall network architecture of a simple centralized whole music system installed in a three bedroom apartment is presented in Figure 6.1.

❏ **Figure 6.1 Three Bedroom Apartment - Centralized Music**

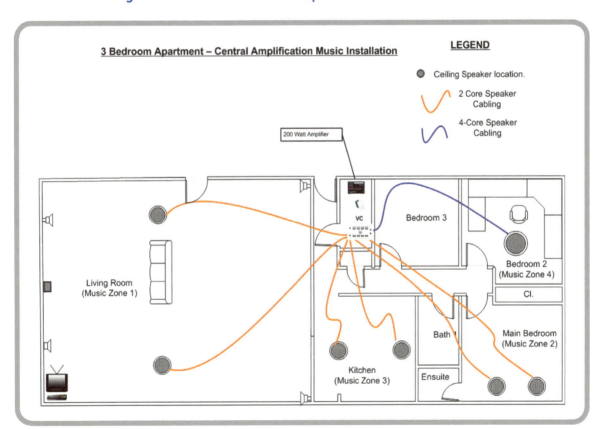

Although the above configuration will work, there are a couple of drawbacks:

 You will not be able to turn the music ON and OFF from each room and you will find yourself heading back to where the amplifier is installed to turn speakers ON and OFF. That's fine for a week or so, but starts to become a hassle after that initial period of time.

You have no way of controlling volume in each of the rooms – which again is annoying.

An enhancement to a centralized multi-room music system that includes some basic volume controls to adjust listening levels in each of the rooms is illustrated in Figure 6.2.

☐ **Figure 6.2: Three Bedroom Apartment - Centralized Music (Individual Volume Controls)**

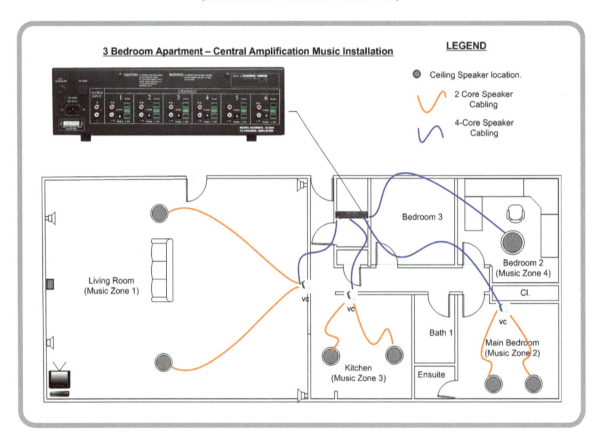

This is the simplest and lowest cost method of sending music around your house.

2. Mid-Level Systems

Moving to the next level of sophistication involves the addition of a localized system for controlling music volume. Nowadays, it is relatively inexpensive to implement a localized volume control system and involves the addition of some extra Category 5e cabling and the installation of wall-mounted keypads:

- **Cat 5e or Cat6 Cabling –** This type of inexpensive cabling is commonly used for computer networking, and an increasing number of self-builders and re-modellers are putting Cat5e cables in as standard parts of their housing developments. With these types of mid-level systems, the Cat5e is used for both carrying the actual music and the associated control data on the one wire.

- **Keypads** – *Wall mounted keypads* control many of the music source's functions. Keypads are normally installed in convenient locations such as near the entrance of a listening zone. For example, most home owners install keypads in close proximity to a doorway. It should be noted that the level of control supported by keypads varies between system suppliers. Most of these keypads include a built-in infrared receiver that allows you to send commands via the amplifier to the music sources.

The installation of an entry and mid-level whole-house audio system with a localized volume control system has a number of benefits:

- These systems simultaneously deliver music to separate rooms within a house.

- Very easy to install and implement.

- Relatively cheap to add to a home design.

Figure 6.3 shows the wiring infrastructure of a popular whole house music system called A-Bus installed in a three bedroom apartment.

❑ **Figure 6.3 – Three Bedroom Apartment – A-Bus Music**

Please note that these wires should really be run during the construction phase of your extension or house.

3. Next Generation MRM 2.0 Systems

> **❝** *iPhone, Android tablets and iPad Apps, remote controls and iPod docking stations are also commonly used with these advanced systems.* **❞**

The most sophisticated type of whole house system is one that is capable of simultaneously delivering music to over six zones from multiple music sources.

As shown in Figure 6.4, individual cat5e cables are run to each of the in-wall volume controls and all speaker wires are home run.

❑ **Figure 6.4 - Three Bedroom Apartment (Multi-Room & Multi Source Music)**

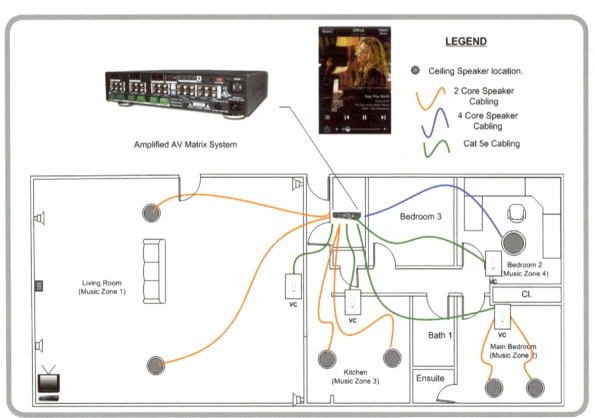

The types of sources supported by these powerful systems range from media centers and tablets to smartphones and Network-Attached Storage (NAS) drives. Advanced control keypads that allow you to read artist, album, song, and track data directly from the user interface are also included with these types of systems.

Next generation MRM 2.0 systems make it possible to enjoy full surround sound from the DVD player in the main sitting room whilst simultaneously sending music from a different source, i.e. a smartphone, to other rooms in the house. So everybody gets a chance to listen to the music that they want to hear without bothering other family members. In addition to sophisticated wall mounted keypads, iPhone, Android tablets and iPad Apps, remote controls and iPod docking stations are also commonly used with these advanced systems. Note that the implementation of sophisticated multi-room sound systems can be expensive and should be fully researched prior to installation.

Planning an MRM 2.0 System

One of the first considerations for anyone thinking about installing a MRM 2.0 system is to identify which rooms you might want to listen to music. Your digital home integrator or electrical contractor should be able to provide guidance on the most suitable areas for the system. The main bedroom, kitchen, living area and main bathroom are some of the more popular locations. This is because these areas are primarily used for relaxation and entertainment. It is also worth bearing in mind that rooms that are part of a MRM system are often referred to as 'zones' and in some cases adjacent rooms can make up a single zone. For instance, the kitchen and dining areas are often configured as a single audio zone. Once a decision has being made on locations it is now time to decide on the type of multi-room sound system that you want to install. This will depend on how the following questions are answered:

① Are you building a new house or retrofitting an existing building?

② How many zones or areas of the house do you want music?

③ Do you want to include an outdoor zone as part of the whole house audio system?

④ Is it likely that family members will listen to different music sources at the same time?

⑤ What level of control should be available in each of the multi-room sound system zones?

⑥ What type of listening will be required in each of the rooms – entertainment or background?

The above questions will help to determine your listening habits. A table included in the workbook section of this chapter will act as an initial guide for ruling in or out certain types of multi-room music systems.

Wireless MRM 2.0 Systems

Until recently, the ability to install a multi-room audio system was really only an option for people building new houses or carrying out major refurbishments in their homes due to the need to install multiple runs of speaker and Cat5e cable. Fortunately this situation has changed with the advent of wireless technologies that allow you to enjoy the benefits of whole house systems without the need to completely re-wire your home.

Steps to Install a Wireless MRM 2.0 System

Here is how you would go putting together a whole house wireless music system without running wires:

STEP 1   Answer Some Basic Questions

For a start do you have a home network connected to a high-speed broadband connection? These connections are required in order to access music services based on the Internet, and personal music you may have stored locally on a hard disk or NAS device. All of the wireless music systems available on the market require Wi-Fi connectivity; thus the need for a home network.

Also, how many rooms are you going to include in your wireless MRM 2.0 system? This will determine the number of wireless music players required for your new system. Many people start off with one room and grow the number of 'music rooms' over time. For instance, if you have a home theatre receiver that you use for playing DVDs then it is possible to interconnect with a wireless music player and incorporate it into your overall wireless whole house music system.

STEP 2   Plan Your Wireless MRM 2.0 System

What types of audio equipment do you already own? This is important because you will want to reuse as much as possible – particularly in these times of austerity! Note them down, as this equipment list will be used as a basis for building out your new whole house wireless music system. Once this information is before us, it will be easier to decide what equipment you need to purchase and configure at home.

Example: Planning a three room wireless system

Tables 6.1 and 6.2 summarize an example requirement and solution to build out a 3 bedroom wireless music system.

❑ **Table 6.1 Inventory of existing music system components**

Room	Pieces of equipment to reuse
Sitting Room	A/V receiver connected to TV and five bookshelf speakers – primarily used for viewing Blu-ray DVDs and cable TV channels
Main bedroom	2 In-ceiling speakers
Kitchen	No equipment

Requirement

Gerard wants to create a wireless music system that will allow him play Internet radio solutions in three separate rooms.

Solution

The following table summarizes the actions that Gerard needs to take to achieve his objective of streaming Internet radio stations into the three rooms.

❑ **Table 6.2 – Proposed Wireless MRM 2.0 Upgrade Actions**

Room	Actions
Sitting Room	Connect a wireless player to either the analog or digital interfaces on the A/V receiver.
Main bedroom	Install a wireless player that includes amplification functionality
Kitchen	Include a wireless player that has in-built speakers and amplification capabilities

STEP 3   Choose a whole house wireless music platform

As described, a wireless MRM 2.0 system consists of players scattered throughout your house. How these players communicate with each other depends on the type of system you decide to purchase. The following table summarizes three different core networking technologies used by Wireless MRM 2.0 system manufacturers:

❏ **Table 6.3 Wireless MRM 2.0 platforms**

Wireless MRM 2.0	Description
SonosNet	Sonos is the undisputed leader of wireless multi-zone music systems. The Sonos MRM 2.0 System is a modular set of players that allow you to play the same or different songs simultaneously throughout the house. The system is pretty straightforward and consists of two product categories, namely wireless music players and controllers. Please also note that Sonos uses a proprietary wireless mesh networking protocol called SonosNet.
Airplay	AirPlay is Apple's wireless technology that may be used to share music between various Apple iOS devices. For example you can use Airplay to stream music from an iPad, iPhone, iPod and a PC with iTunes to a growing range of Airplay enabled products ranging from iPod docks to AV receivers and speakers. Setting up an MRM 2.0 system based on Airplay is pretty straightforward. One of the simplest examples of how easy it is to setup an Airplay MRM 2.0 system involves an Apple device called an Airport, which is plugged into your power socket. The AirPort includes an audio out, which gets connected to a pair of speakers. Once the hardware is in place, then launch an iPhone app called 'Remote' and the AirPort appears on the screen as a receiving device for your iTunes music library. Although Airplay is great, it does have one or two drawbacks that are worth noting: An iPad or iPhone can only control one Airplay device at any one time. Each Airplay zone in your house plays the same music, so is not fully classified as a full blown multi-source and multi-zone wireless MRM 2.0 system.
DLNA	Although less popular for true MRM 2.0 applications, a technology called DLNA, which stands for Digital Living Network Alliance can also be used to wirelessly transmit music around the house.

STEP 4 **Install & Configure**

Installing and configuration techniques will vary depending on the type of system you choose to purchase. Step-by-step instructions on how to install Sonos and Airplay MRM 2.0 wireless MRM systems are available inside my video course.

Add Music to Your Garden

> **"** *With family and friends around, high quality outdoor garden speakers are often used to create that instant party atmosphere!* **"**

Outdoor entertaining has become increasingly popular in recent years. With access to so much music on your smartphone or online why should it only be available indoors? With family and friends around, high quality outdoor garden speakers are often used to create that instant party atmosphere! Adding an outdoor area to a music system involves the creation of an extra zone that involves the installation of weatherproof speakers. One of the great things about outdoor speakers is that they can be installed virtually anywhere in your garden.

There are a myriad of outdoor speaker options designed to meet the needs of consumers. They come in various shapes and colors in order to blend in with the landscape. You can choose between the traditional design, high performance speakers that attach to a wall or, the increasingly popular and reasonably priced 'Rock' speakers that blend discreetly into your garden landscape. In addition to varying form factors, outdoor speakers are also available for both wired and wireless retrofit install situations. The following sections explain in more detail:

Wired Outdoor Speakers

As the name suggests, wired outdoor speakers are weatherproof and are connected to your centralized MRM system with a cable. Typical characteristics include:

- No electricity is required as the power is transmitted over the speaker cable.

- The music gets reproduced pretty accurately because there is no interference on the cable that could degrade music quality.

Here are the three main steps you need to take to install and setup some wired outdoor speakers:

STEP 1 Finalize Two Locations for your Pair of Wired Outdoor Speakers

In an outdoor environment the dispersion of sound is different compared to inside. Therefore, placing speakers relatively close to the listening area is important. As a rule of thumb, I would typically try to locate speakers approximately 10 to 15 feet away from the listening area (e.g. a seated location or a BBQ).

STEP 2 Run Speaker cable

As shown in Figure 6.5, you now need to run two-core well insulated speaker cable, some from wherever in the garden you plan to locate the outdoor speakers back to your existing speaker source – i.e. some type of amplifier.

> **! Quick Side Note from ● Gerard:**
>
> I'd be inclined to install the left and right outdoor speakers between 6 and 10 feet apart.

❏ **Figure 6.5 Outdoor speakers wiring infrastructure**

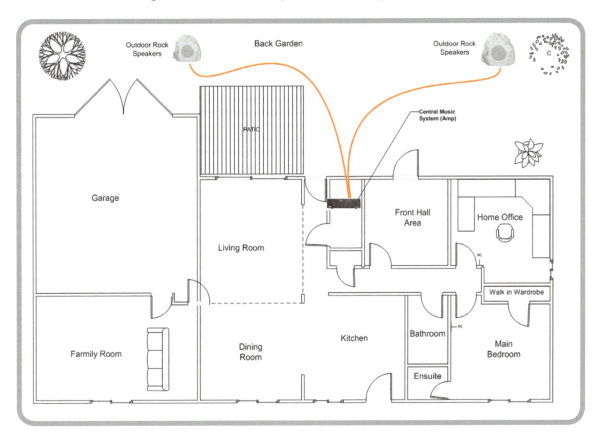

That means getting the cable through some outside walls and into the house! This type of installation is messy and might involve help from a local handyman or builder.

STEP 3 **Connect speakers to your music source**

Once you have identified an ideal location for your outdoor speakers and pre-wired accordingly, wall speakers will need to be mounted, rock speakers will be just placed on the ground and all cables will be terminated.

!Quick Side Note from ●Gerard:

Try and source some direct burial speaker cable as it is designed to operate in difficult environmental conditions underground.

Wireless Outdoor Speakers

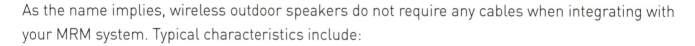

As the name implies, wireless outdoor speakers do not require any cables when integrating with your MRM system. Typical characteristics include:

- Wireless outdoor speakers can either use Infrared or long range RF signals to communicate with the music source. RF based outdoor speakers have an obvious advantage in the sense that they do not require line of sight, which will be the case for 90% of installations.

- No need to plan or install new cables; thus you will have greater flexibility in terms of locating the units exactly where you want them.

- They include an in-built amplifier and receiver – batteries are required to provide power.

- Wireless outdoor speakers are prone to interference from external sources from time to time.

- Transmission distances will vary, depending on the number of obstructions blocking the signal between the transmitter plugged into your MRM system and the outdoor wireless speakers.

Here are the two main steps you need to take to install and setup some wireless outdoor speakers:

STEP 1
Finalize Two Locations for your Pair of Wireless Outdoor Speakers

Because wireless speakers in general have less power than their wired counterparts, I would be inclined to locate within 5 or 7 feet of your listening area.

STEP 2
Connect the Wireless Music Transmitter to your MRM System

Plug in the transmission unit and connect with your music source using standard A/V cables. That's it!

Which to choose – Wired or Wireless Outdoor Speakers?

If you don't want the hassle of running outdoor speaker cable or maybe it's not physically possible, then you may want to consider using some wireless speakers to extend your MRM system out into the garden or back yard. It is hard to beat the sound that comes from an outdoor wired speaker when compared to its wireless counterpart, however the convenience of having a simple install may in some cases sway people towards using wireless technologies in their back gardens.

Practical Usage Example

MRM 2.0 systems are quite powerful and provide some great automation features. Here is a simple example of how we use our MRM 2.0 system in the mornings.

Getting ourselves out of bed in the morning is challenging on these cold Irish mornings! Try adding five young children to the mix and it becomes a major challenge to mobilize everyone down to the kitchen for breakfast ☺ So during the weekdays, I have programmed our MRM 2.0 system as follows:

 Activate music alarm on weekdays only. We like to have a sleep-in over the weekend ☺

I have the system setup to start playing music through the in-ceiling speakers in our own room, the kids' room and the kitchen at 7:15 and finishing at 8:45.

③ I like to wakeup to Newstalk in the morning! The kids or Olive prefer TodayFM; so the playlist setting changes on a regular basis ☺

Another handy automated function of MRM 2.0 systems is that they also allow you to have the music you are listening to automatically turn OFF after a set amount of time – useful at bedtime.

Things to Remember

Inside this chapter you learned about both wireless and wired MRM 2.0 systems – here are the key take away points to remember:

- There are three different levels of wired based house music systems to choose from, make sure you understand the differences.

- Entry level whole house music systems utilize speaker cable only and have limited control capabilities.

- Mid-level whole house music systems are normally controlled via wall mounted keypads only. They are relatively cheap to incorporate as part of a new build construction project and allow you to listen to different songs in different rooms.

- Next generation MRM 2.0 are typically controlled via a mobile device such as a smartphone or tablet, are more expensive to buy and support a ton of features!

- Overall wireless MRM 2.0 systems are still a fairly young product and dominated by a US based company called Sonos. There are other potential players in this space such as Apple's Airplay, Google Nexus... and a new solution from Casatunes; but for the moment, Sonos remains the dominant platform in the M2M 2.0 marketplace.

- Outdoor entertainment speakers allow you to enjoy listening to music, regardless of the weather!

- MRM systems can be configured to gently wake you up in the morning by playing your favorite Internet radio station through your bedroom speakers.

Now that you understand how to install both wired and wireless MRM 2.0 systems, you're ready to move on to another one of my favourite HA 2.0 functions – Viewing awesome HDTV content in every room of your home!

Okay, ready for some HDTV!

CHAPTER 7

STEP 5: ADD WHOLE HOUSE HDTV DISTRIBUTION TO YOUR HA 2.0 SYSTEM

HDTV Introduction

Before discussing how to send full High Definition (HD) quality picture and sound around your house, it is first helpful to provide an overview of HDTV. Next generation HDTV channels are revolutionising the transmission and reception of video services. HDTV has finally arrived and is here to stay. There are a number of reasons why consumers are flocking to the technology. The following is a short list of the most compelling ones:

Improvement in video quality: The evolution from traditional analog TV to digital TV has already provided consumers with sharper, richer and more engaging video content. Migrating from standard digital TV to HDTV represents the next significant trend currently happening in the TV world.

Widescreen Picture – Unlike analog's square picture, HDTV's widescreen format offers viewers a more theater-like experience. The widescreen format provides a wider image area that more closely matches the movie theatre experience. Best of all, when viewed on a widescreen display, consumers won't experience black bars (letterboxing) or a stretched picture.

Better color resolution – The color resolution supported by HDTV is far superior to the resolution of regular standard digital video content. In fact, HDTV offers resolutions up to five times that of analog TV, as well as remarkable improvements in brightness and color depth. The incredibly detailed, life-like pictures make viewers feel like part of the action.

Spectacular Surround Sound – Like DVD, many HDTV programs such as sporting events, sitcoms, dramas or feature movies are all presented in Dolby® Digital surround sound.

Before going into the nuts and bolts of setting up your HDTV distribution system, let me first introduce the protocol or standard used to transmit digital HDTV signals – HDMI

HDMI Overview

HDMI (High-Definition Multimedia Interface) is defined as a digital connectivity technology that is used to transmit uncompressed data, video and audio signals over a single cable. From a practical perspective it consists of yet another A/V interface that replaces the plethora of analog interfaces integrated into the current crop of consumer electronic devices. Specialized HDMI cables are used to interconnect high-definition A/V sources such as set-top boxes, Apple TV, DVD players, game consoles, home theatre receivers and even iPads with display devices such as flat screen TVs, projectors, and computer monitors.

In the world of HDMI, electronic devices are categorized:

- *HDMI Sources* store and send HD video content. Set-top boxes Blu-ray DVD players, media streamers, and projectors are all examples.

- As the name implies *HDMI splitters* allows you to use a single HDMI source and split the output signal between multiple HDTVs simultaneously.

- *HDMI Switches* allows you to connect multiple HDMI sources to a single TV – the opposite of what a HDMI splitter is used for!

- *HDMI Matrixes* are the most sophisticated of all the HDMI devices available on the market. They allow you to route any HDMI source to any TV display.

Various Approaches to Distributing HDTV Content to Multiple Rooms

There are two main reasons why you might want to install a HDTV distribution system:

 A HDTV distribution system is cheaper than buying multiple HD source devices for each room.

 Although most HD installations are limited to a single room, there is an appetite within many families around the world to have some flexibility in terms of what is watched on each of the TVs around the house. For instance, in our case myself and Olive like to watch shows like the Apprentice and Dragon's Den; this bores the kids, so they use our HDTV distribution system to watch some Disney Channel content on another TV located in our 'play room'.

Most typical homes have an existing coaxial infrastructure, which is not really fit for purpose when it comes to installing a HDTV distribution system. The cable is generally of poor quality and run in a daisy chain fashion.

Thus, in order to route high definition audio/video from any of your HD video sources to TV displays in different rooms you will need to send the signal over a particular media type, namely HDMI cables, Cat5e/Cat6 cables, wirelessly, over your in-home electrical wires or over your existing coaxial cables.

Using Native HDMI Cabling to build a Multi-Zone HDTV Distribution System

HDMI cables are now the standard for all in-home AV installations and running a single HDMI cable from a central location to each of the rooms simplifies your cabling requirements and eliminates the maze of cables required by the various types of analog interfaces.

Using HDMI cables to provide access to centralized HDTV content sources in a number of rooms around your house is an ideal scenario, because these cables were designed specifically for this function.

Unfortunately, there are some limitations that you need to be aware of before going online and buying a bunch of HDMI cables of varying lengths.

① For a start, HDMI was originally designed and intended to interconnect local pieces of AV equipment together in a single room.

② There may be a long distance between where your HD video sources are located and some of the rooms. HDMI cables have limited transmission capabilities and have difficulties in sending HD content over long distances.

③ High quality HDMI cables are typically quite expensive to buy – particularly lengths of 10 metres and above.

④ HDMI cables are difficult to repair if they get damaged during construction.

⑤ Even terminating HDMI cables is challenging. It's generally hard to come up with an exact measurement of cable between where the final location for the HD source equipment will be and the TVs located in the various rooms. From an installer perspective it is quite possible that you could end up tie wrapping excess cables behind the TV!

Over the past two years, the video industry has released a number of HD distribution products that are designed to overcome the limitations of using HDMI native cables to distribute HD content around a building.

Building a Cat5e/6 based HDTV Distribution System Overview

Cat5e and Cat6 cables have become the standard means of building whole house HDTV systems in recent times.

There are four steps associated with installing a system that utilizes Cat 5e and preferably Cat 6 cables to distribute HDTV signals around the house:

STEP 1

Run one and possibly two lengths of standard Cat 5e/6 cable from a central point in your home to each existing or potential TV location. A rack with your HD source equipment is normally located at this centralized area.

STEP 2

These cables are subsequently terminated on an HDMI matrix, which should be mounted inside your rack.

STEP 3

In addition to terminating the Cat6s at the HDMI matrix, your HD sources are also connected to the matrix via short HDMI patch leads. So once you press play on your DVD player, the signal is sent out of the HDMI port, into the HDMI matrix, transmitted over along the Cat6 cable until it reaches one of the remote rooms.

STEP 4

At the remote room a HDMI receiver is used to interface with the Cat5e/6. This unit typically requires a local power socket and its

> ## !Quick Side Note from Gerard:
> ●Good quality Cat6 cable should be used where possible. Remember this stuff is going inside your walls and cannot be easily replaced! I have seen projects where the homeowner has spent thousands of Euros on a multi-room entertainment system, yet ends up getting his electrician to run cheap Cat5 cable, which does not support the high data rate requirements of HDMI.

main function is to send a signal out its port, over the HDMI patch lead connected to the HDMI input port on your HDTV.

It is worth noting that the video is transmitted in an uncompressed format and the picture you see on the TV is the same as if you had the HDMI cable connected directly between the DVD player and the HDTV – no loss in quality.

Enter HDBaseT

"It is now possible to send HDMI over a single Cat6 cable."

Up to recently, HDMI matrixes required two Cat6 cables at each of the remote rooms to support transmission of the HDTV signal. With the advent of a newer version of HDMI called HDBaseT; it is now possible to send HDMI over a single Cat6 cable.

From a technical perspective:

- HDbaseT matrix products are based on HDMI 1.4 and support advanced video technologies such as 3D, higher resolutions and deep color.

- Power of Ethernet is supported by HDBaseT; thus no need for additional power leads at each of the TV locations.

- From a control perspective IR passthrough is a standard feature, which allows you to control your HDMI sources as if you were sitting right in front of the devices.

- As an added bonus HDBaseT products also supports 100 Mbps Ethernet, which provides fast Internet connectivity to each of your rooms in addition to crisp HDTV pictures!

❑ **Figure 7.1 Four source, four output HDBaseT distribution System**

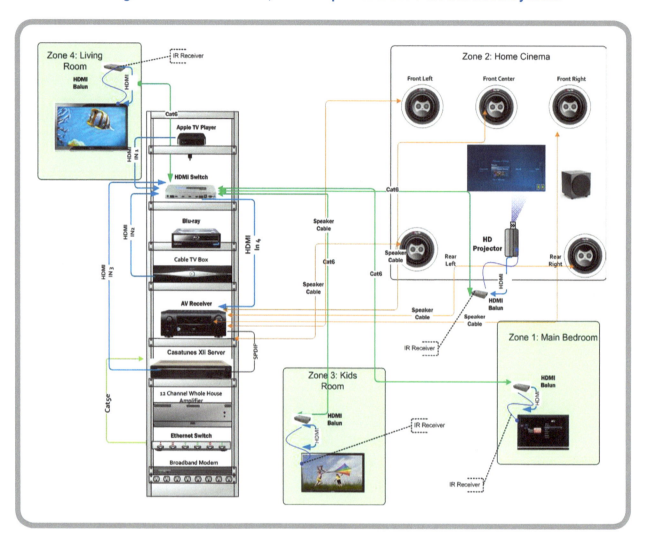

Figure 7.1 illustrates the use of HDBase-T in distributing 4 HD sources, namely an Apple TV media streamer, a regular HD Cable TV box, a Blu-ray player and a HD media server to the following rooms:

① Main Bedroom

② Home Cinema room

③ Kids Room

④ Living Room

As shown, a single Cat 6 cable is run to each TV location, where it is terminated on a HDMI balun, which then connects to the display or projector using a short HDMI patch lead.

Although, HDMI or Cat5e/6 cabling are popular methods for building an end-to-end HDTV entertainment solution, there are some drawbacks, namely:

- Running cabling can be expensive, especially if walls need to be cut and repaired afterwards.

- It may be expensive and impractical to run cable to certain parts of your home – over a fireplace or outside to the garden are two prime examples.

- If the cable is damaged, it can be difficult to open up the walls and fix the problem.

- The final location of your screen will be dictated by the cable point of termination, often making optimal viewing placement a problem.

In order to overcome some of these issues, the market has responded by creating two types of HDTV distribution systems that do not require running cable, namely wireless and Powerline.

Whole House Wireless HDTV Distribution Systems Overview

As described above, there are some limitations when it comes to running cable in a building. Thus HDTV systems that utilize the airwaves have started to grow in popularity over the past couple of years. The principle advantages of wireless based HDTV distribution systems include:

These systems are based on radio frequencies – thus line of sight is not required. RF based systems are capable of sending signals through doors, walls, floors and ceilings. Thus, you will be able to locate your HD source equipment out of view.

If a problem occurs, troubleshooting is easy because there is no need to re-open walls and trace cables.

Improved flexibility and portability in terms of locating your TV screen or projector.

No need to drill holes and run cables through walls.

IR support allows you to control HD source equipment.

The following are technical characteristics of wireless HDTV systems:

They utilize unlicensed radio frequencies (some form of Wi-Fi) and can operate at reasonably long distances.

A wireless HD system consists of a transmitter and one or more receivers. A wireless HD transmitter broadcasting full HD video and audio to four separate receivers is represented graphically in Figure 7.2.

❑ **Figure 7.2 Whole House Wireless HDTV Distribution System**

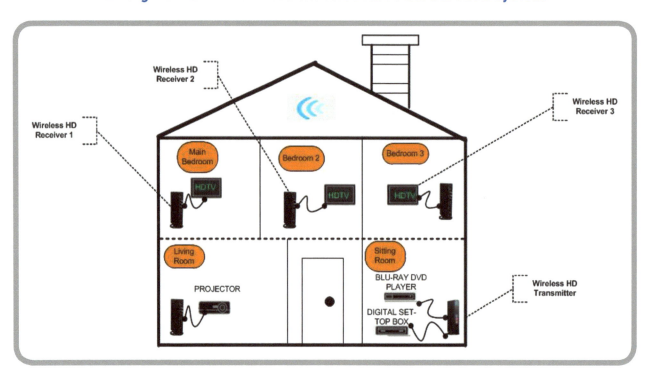

• • • • • • ● They are capable of transmitting HD content at high quality, namely 1080p.

• • • • • • ● Multiple HD source connectivity is typically supported by the transmitter.

• • • • • • ● Two-way communication is supported between the transmitter and the receivers.

Installation is pretty straightforward and typically involves the following steps:

① Simply plug your HDTV into the receiver via an HDMI cable.

② Connect up to 4 HD source devices into the Wireless HDMI transmitter unit.

③ Power up your HDTV and start watching HD or 3D video content!

Although Wireless HDTV systems eliminate cable clutter and their reliability has improved in recent times, the widespread retrofitting of wireless HDTV has not occurred due to lack of standards, high costs and of course glitches in picture quality that occur during periods of interference.

Powerline HDTV Distribution Systems Overview

The possibility of routing HD video over your existing in-home power cables holds some promise for people who want to avoid the hassles of running new Cat5e/6 cable and are not comfortable with using wireless technologies. Here are some specific installs that opted for Powerline over wireless:

A customer based in the UK lives in an old farmhouse built with stone and some of the walls are over a meter thick. Wireless would not have been able to penetrate these walls, so he opted to purchase a Powerline kit and the solution works perfectly fine.

Another customer of ours who owns a pub here in Ireland wanted to add a waterproof TV to an outside area.

The following are characteristics of Powerline HDTV systems:

A basic Powerline HD kit consists of a transmitter that sends out the HD signals and a receiver, which is connected to the HDTV.

Provides HDTV connectivity between sources such as digital set-top boxes, gaming units and Blu-ray™ disc players to HDMI compatible TV displays.

The receiver units require local power at the HDTV display.

Based on a technology called HomePlug AV.

Capable of supporting up to 4 separate receivers.

Similar to cable and wireless based systems, Powerline HDTV systems also support IR control.

Distributing HDTV over Powerline is in its infancy, however I did receive a HDTV Powerline kit from a UK supplier and setup in my own house according to the diagram shown in Figure 7.3.

❏ **Figure 7.3 HD over Powerline Network Architecture**

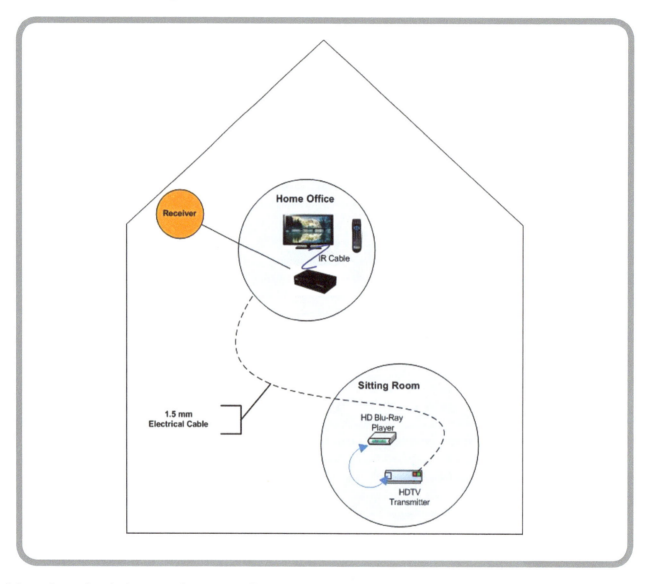

It did work perfectly from a picture quality perspective and the ability to remotely control my HD Blu-ray player using IR pass through worked well. Here are some of my personal observations about using Powerline as a means of building a whole house HDTV system:

① The technology is relatively new and is unproven because it has not yet achieved significant market penetration.

② The physical sizes of the receiver units are large and a little clunky.

③ Although, no expensive rewiring is required Powerline HDTV distribution systems remain confined to specialized commercial and residential installations at the time of writing.

Things to Remember

In this chapter you learned about distributing HDTV around your home, namely using native HDMI cabling, Cat5e/6, wireless or Powerline technologies – here are the key take away points to remember:

- HDMI Splitters, HDMI Switches and HDMI Matrixes are used to route HDTV signals between sources and TV displays.

- From a cabling perspective, there are various networking components available that allow you to send HDMI over four different media types, namely, native HDMI cables, Cat5e/6 cabling, wirelessly and high voltage in-home electrical cable.

- Sending HDTV content within a single room works fine for the most part, problems can arise when it comes to multi-room HDTV systems.

- Cat6 structured cabling infrastructure is typically used as a basis for building most whole house HDTV systems. Installing Cat6 in your home requires a substantial amount of work and really only suits if you are doing some major renovations or building a new house.

- Wireless HDMI kits are an option in locations where it is impractical to run Cat5e/6 cable. Due to distance limitations Wireless HDMI kits are more suited to single room solutions.

- Powerline HDTV kits support the broadcasting of HDTV content to multiple TVs and projectors.

Now that you understand how to view 3D and HD movies in every room of your house, you're now ready to move on to some more content that enhances entertainment in your family's life – Building a Home Cinema!

Okay, ready for some 5 or 7.1!

CHAPTER 8

STEP 6: ADD A HOME CINEMA TO YOUR HA 2.0 SYSTEM

Configuring an area in your home to support a home cinema will be an impressive addition to your home automation system. For years, the home cinema experience was confined to affluent professionals. This is no longer the case with home cinema systems now becoming affordable to larger portions of our population. Also known as a home theater, the extent of your installation can range from a compact surround system that you connect with your TV to a more extensive configuration that involves a dedicated room, a drop down screen, a projector, blackout blinds and more!

This chapter explores how to build a place somewhere in your home where you can relax and enjoy HD quality TV shows and movies!

What's Needed for a Home Cinema System?

Up to recently, people in general were hesitant about dedicating a single room in their homes for the purpose of watching movies. And rightly so – property is expensive. So the compromise is to now call one of an area in your house the 'home cinema room'; but instead of using it solely for the purposes of watching awesome 3D and high definition video content, the area gets used for other day to day activities. My wife uses our home cinema space to dry clothes some days ☺.

On a more serious front, there is more to building a proper home theater system than locating a DVD player in the corner of the room and trailing the cables across a floor to the surround sound speakers!

As illustrated in Figure 8.1 a fully implemented 5.1 home theater system consists of five major components, including:

❏ **Figure 8.1 Home Theater 5.1 System Setup**

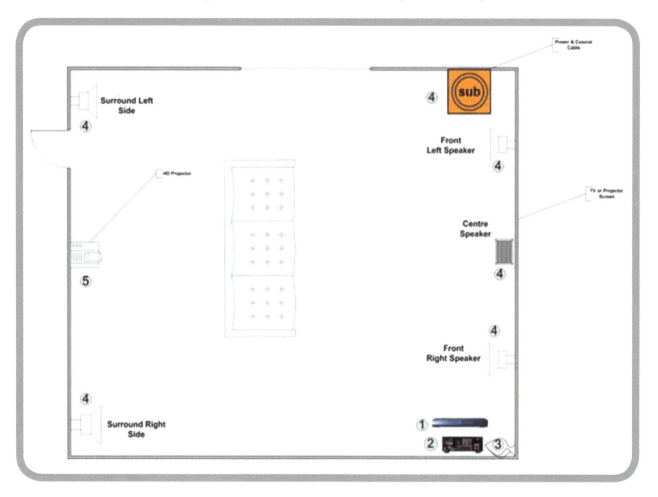

An outline of each component is described below.

① HD Video Content Sources

The core of your end-to-end home cinema system is the actual content you plan to watch. There are several HD sources to choose from that stream HD and 3D TV content, including:

- Blu-ray players

- Streaming media players such as Apple TV

- Satellite set-top boxes

- Media servers

- Home Cinema A/V Receiver

This electronics device connects over HDMI patch leads to your various A/V sources and over cable to your various home cinema speakers. The main functions provided by an A/V receiver include:

- Amplifying the audio received from your content sources and sending out to the correct speakers.

- Route the video content directly to a TV display or projector.

- Allow you to use an app or remote control to select a particular content source for viewing on the screen.

In addition to these core functions, receivers can also incorporate support for a range of emerging digital home technologies, namely:

Apple's Airplay is a protocol that lets you wirelessly stream music from your iPhone, iTunes library or iPad to devices such as A/V receivers and speakers that include the technology.

3D allows you to enjoy movies that are created in this format.

A/V receivers that support *7.1* multichannel sound technologies are able to send out sound to 8 different speakers in your home cinema room, namely left, right, center, left surround, right surround, left rear, right rear and subwoofer positions.

Network connectivity Ethernet and Wi-Fi capabilities lets you play online digital content.

Pretty much all receivers come with their very own App, allowing you to use an iPhone, Android smartphone or tablet to perform control operations such as:

- Powering the unit on and off.

- Switching HDMI sources.

- Turning volumes up and down.

② A Structured Wiring System

This home theatre component is probably the most critical part of the overall system. Implementation is relatively simple and involves the running of 14 gauge speaker cable from a home theater main plate to each of the in-wall or in-ceiling speaker points in the room. Also note that your sub-woofer requires good-quality audio cable and a power socket. Poor quality cable is susceptible to electrical interference and should be avoided!

③ Speakers

Typically, most of the home theater systems available on the high street are capable of at least supporting 5.1 channel digital surround sound. Speakers are at the heart of any home theater system and they fall into three broad categories:

- **On-wall or bookcase speakers –** Decision factors that you need to bear in mind when choosing on-wall speaker or bookcase speakers include price, the number of speakers required for a room, and quality requirements.

- **In wall or in-ceiling speakers –** In-wall speakers are typically installed when you get an opportunity to run speaker cable during a new-build or when re-decorating parts of your building. This speaker category is less invasive than on wall speakers and is often painted to ensure that they blend with the décor of the room. The quality of this speaker category is continuously evolving and improving.

- A subwoofer is also required to process and extend the low frequency base signals emanating from the source equipment.

Having decided on an appropriate speaker form factor that suits the décor of the room, you now need to finalize the location for each of the speakers.

A 5.1 home theater setup consist of the following:

A center speaker who's purpose is to output approximately 50% of a movie's soundtrack, including the dialogue element of the content. As the name implies this speaker is typically installed immediately below or indeed above the center of your TV or projector screen.

Front left and right speakers process the special effects elements of a soundtrack and add realism to the movie experience. These speakers are normally positioned at ear level when seated and an equidistant distance from the center speaker left and right of your screen. Furthermore, front speakers may also be used for listening to music. It is important to note that in most installs the left and right speakers should be, if at all possible at least 5 feet apart (1.5 meters for us Europeans!).

Two Surround sound speakers enrich the movie experience by playing out a variety of atmospheric sounds. With a 5.1 speaker configuration, these speakers are typically located towards the back of your home cinema room. Many of the newer A/V receivers support 4 surround sound speakers. The additional two speakers are ideally placed at ear level at the side of you seating location.

A graphical overview of an 'ideal' speaker layout for a 7.1 system is presented in Figure 8.2.

❑ **Figure 8.2 Architecture of a 7.1 Home Cinema System**

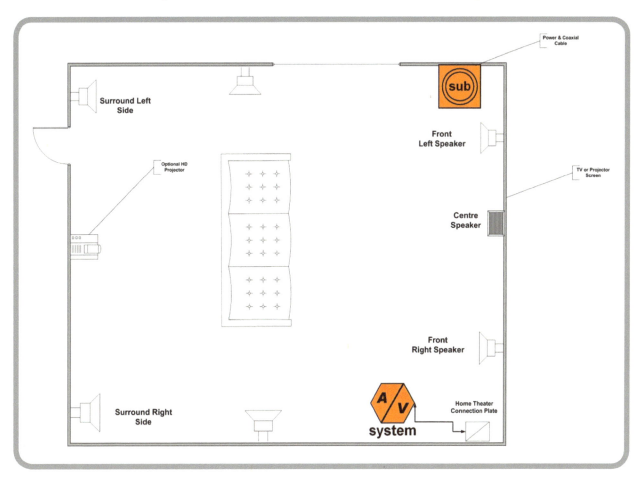

Of course in the real world there are lots of instances where the layout and orientation of rooms do not match the preferred locations for your 5.1 speakers. For instance, in our own sitting room we have the 'TV in the corner' in our sitting room – sound familiar ☺. Here is the layout we use in our L-shaped multi-purpose sitting room that provides us with excellent surround sound.

❏ **Figure 8.3 O'Driscoll's Sitting Room with TV in the Corner**

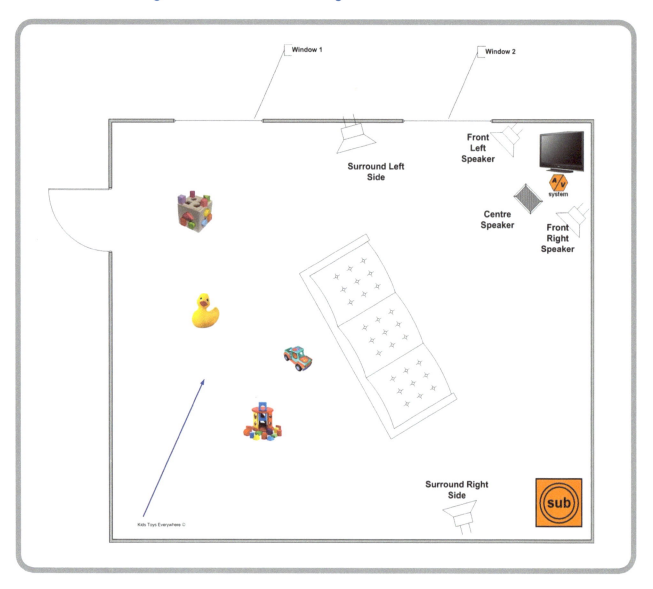

And yes the corner is as cluttered as it appears in the diagram!

A powered subwoofer delivers the base low frequency audio component and makes the movie experience more lifelike. Subwoofers really come into their own during scenes that include special effects such as explosions and storms. The subwoofer gives you the feeling of being right in the middle of the action. Positioning of the sub-woofer can be reasonably flexible – typically plugged in at a corner of the room or a few inches away from one of the four walls.

All of the above speakers work in a cohesive manner to create a surround sound experience when sitting down watching a movie.

④ A Video display

Driven by falling prices and room-friendly dimensions the market for flat panel displays is the fastest growing category within the consumer electronics marketplace. There are a wide variety of sizes and brands to choose from. With regards to preparing your room for a flat screen, it is important to decide on a particular wall location for hanging the flat-panel TV. The preparation of the wall space involves the location of electrical outlets, Cat 5e, and RG-6 outlets in close proximity or directly behind the proposed location of the video display.

Alternatively, some people opt to install a projector instead of a standard flat screen TV. There are a couple of factors that you might want to consider when it comes to choosing one over the other, namely:

- Replacement projector bulbs are expensive. Extended periods of watching live TV will decrease the lifespan of a bulb. This is not an issue for standard flat screen TVs.

- A projector can be used to produce a large video image that spans several feet across and looks much more impressive when compared to a standard large screen TV. Therefore, projectors are ideal for watching HD movies whereas standard TVs are more suited to the day-to-day patterns of watching regular TV.

Combining the above building blocks together will allow you to enjoy and experience the full benefits of home cinema technologies.

⑤ Wi-Fi to IR Systems

Imagine replacing the remote controls that accompany the various components used to build your home cinema with a sleek and attractive iPhone, iPad, Windows 8 or Android tablet app.

By integrating a Wi-Fi to infrared (IR) remote system with a HA 2.0 controller your smartphone or tablet turns into a handy and comfortable universal remote control!

In addition to replacing piles of remote controls, home automation controllers can run scenes that execute a number of instructions – simplifying life for you. For instance, Wi-Fi to IR control units let you tap a 'Watch TV' App icon and the automation system takes care of the rest. What I mean by taking care of the rest is executing a bunch of commands. For example it could involve the following:

- Diming the lights

- Lowering the blackout blinds

- Turning the set-top box ON

- Changing to your favorite TV channel

Other features supported by these systems include the ability to:

- Control your A/V equipment from anywhere in the world

- Integrate with your home automation alarm system, so when an intruder breaks in, get your home automation controller to turn on music in the home cinema room – really loud!

- Automatically turn off A/V equipment at a pre-set time or when the room is unoccupied.

- Customize the look and feel of the various icons on your iPhone, Windows 8 or Android App.

How Wi-fi to IR units work?

Similar to IR remotes; Wi-Fi universal remotes also send wireless signals through the air. The big advantage of a Wi-Fi remote over their IR counterparts is their ability to travel through walls and solid objects.

As the name implies Wi-Fi universal remotes are controlled over a Wi-Fi network from users' smartphones, tablets or computers, and are more flexible than handheld universal remotes. As well as eliminating the need for other remote controls they can be controlled from anywhere in the home without requiring a line-of-sight.

❏ **Figure 8.4 Basic Wi-Fi to IR Basic Network Architecture**

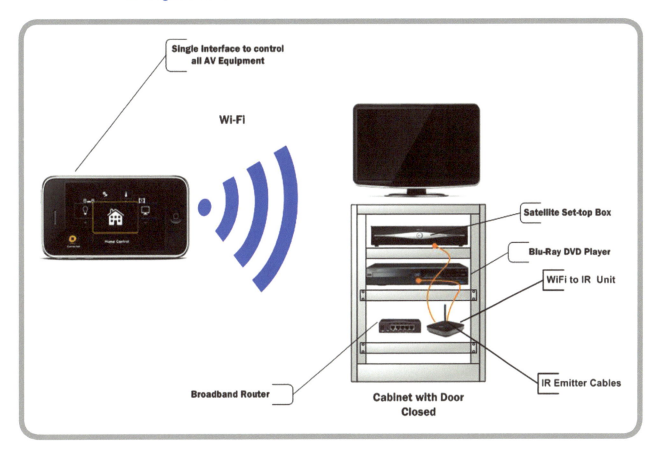

As shown in Figure 8.4; a basic Wi-Fi to IR system comprises a hardware device and a software app that turns your iPhone, iPad or Android device into a universal remote control.

The hardware device, also known as the Wi-Fi to IR controller, is at the heart of these systems and is connected to your home Wi-Fi network. It is normally located next to your AV equipment in a cabinet to reduce room clutter. The main function of the Wi-Fi to IR control unit is to accept commands, look up an IR code database and broadcast IR commands to your various AV devices. LEDs positioned on the unit are used to emit these IR commands. Each LED has an effective range of between 35 and 40 feet.

Tip: Use the IR learning feature to capture codes for particular brands of equipment that are not stored in the Wi-Fi control unit.

Wi-Fi to IR systems also includes a software app that acts as a centralized graphical user interface. Without this element of the system, there is a likelihood that you could end up switching between multiple apps in order to control each individual item of AV equipment. In this single-room example for instance three separate apps may be used to control the Blu-ray DVD player, satellite set-top box and TV.

More advanced Wi-Fi to IR systems, such as the one shown in Figure 8.5 provide support for third party serial and contact closures which allow you to control other systems such as motorized blinds and lighting panels.

❏ **Figure 8.5 Advanced Wi-Fi to IR Basic Network Architecture**

Installing a Wi-Fi to IR unit

Installing this device is pretty straight forward and typically involves the following steps:

 Power up the unit.

 Connect to your Home Wi-Fi network.

③   Open the default setup screen in a PC or tablet browser.

④   Download and configure your App as needed.

The full instructions on how to install and configure a Wi-Fi to IR unit are rather visual, it's better presented with a video. Inside my video course, I show you exactly how to setup one of these amazing remote controls units in your home.

Wi-Fi to IR System Drawbacks

While tablet devices such as iPads and Kindle Fires can offer you a fantastic interface to control your AV equipment, there are some challenges associated with using a tablet as the main remote control:

- Tablets are quite large and it can feel a little strange at first because we are all programmed to use hard button remotes when changing TV channels.

- Some of our customers prefer using hard buttons to navigate their TV channel list.

- Our iPad has a habit of going missing every so often and we find it in one of the kids bedrooms. Also remotes get used a lot and in our own case, our three year old has bounced the unit off the floor on occasions.

In my opinion the benefits of using Wi-Fi to IR systems far outweigh the challenges listed above.

Lower Cost Home Cinema Control Option!

Please also note that if your control requirements are less sophisticated and you have line of sight with your home cinema equipment then consideration should be given to using an IR dongle. These units attach directly to your smartphone and are a great option for basic control of your AV equipment. By downloading and installing an App your iOS or Android device is converted into a universal remote control within minutes. These IR dongles are pretty cheap and work perfectly if you have direct line of sight with your AV equipment.

Adding Automation to your Home Cinema

There is more to a cinema experience besides sound and video signals. Aspects such as mood lighting, blackout blinds and ensuring the room temperature is comfortable all help to enhance the home cinematic experience.

HA 2.0 systems can be used to integrate your home cinema AV equipment and automate the following activities:

Lighting – Use the power of your home automation controller and install one or two wireless lighting control modules to add ambiance to your home cinema room or area.

Blind & curtain control - Tapping an icon on your smarphone or tablet to close your window blinds or curtains would be a nice touch when initially sitting down to watch a movie.

Heating control - Use your smartphone or tablet to increase room temperature; without getting off the couch

Practical Usage Example

Requirement

A homeowner living in Germany who had previously purchased an HA 2.0 controller back in 2011, reconnected with us over email a while back and was looking for an elegant solution that would allow him to re-locate his AV home theater receiver and Blu-ray player from his sitting room to a separate area in the house – the utility room.

Although the move improves aesthetics in the sitting room, the equipment would no longer be within line of sight, thus our client required a solution that allowed him to remotely control his AV equipment at the new location.

In addition to relocating his AV gear, the homeowner also wanted to configure a scene on the controller to dim the lights and lower the motorized blinds when sitting down to watch a movie.

Here is the solution that was proposed and used:

The Solution

The items of equipment installed are illustrated in Figure 8.6.

❑ Figure 8.6 Adding Automation to a Home Theater Setup

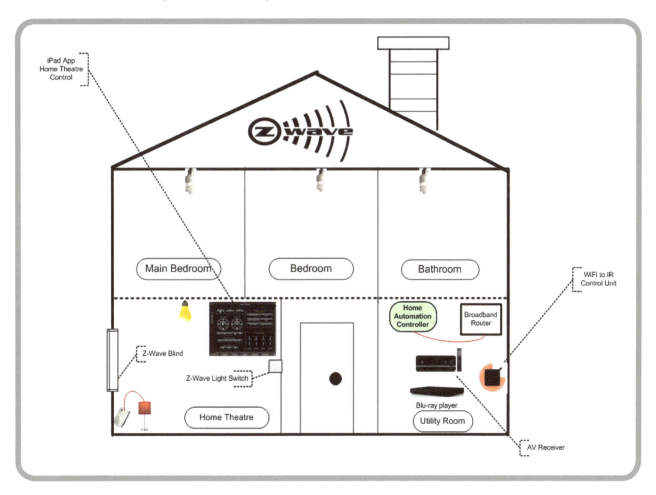

As illustrated, the homeowner bought and installed the following items:

①   A Wi-Fi-to-IR bridge control unit.

②   Z-Wave controlled electric blinds.

③   A Z-Wave enabled light switch.

④   A customizable application that turns his smartphone into a universal remote control.

Things to Remember

In this chapter, here are the key take points to remember:

● Home cinema systems are becoming more affordable.

● Wi-Fi to IR blasters allow for the control of multiple AV devices and are operated via an iOS, Windows or Android App.

FINAL THOUGHTS

Now that you understand what's needed to build an end-to-end HA 2.0 system; you now need to start building out your own system.

Table 8.3 below provides you with a summarized action plan, which you can follow over the coming weeks, months and indeed years.

❑ **Table 1.0 – Building your own HA 2.0 System Blueprint**

1.0	**Improve your Families Security & Safety Levels**	**o**
1.1	Buy a home controller security kit	o
1.2	Setup your Absence & Alarm Systems	o
1.3	Install a HA 2.0 smoke & fire detection system	o
1.4	Configure one or multiple IP cameras and interfaces with your HA 2.0 controller	o
2.0	**Integrate home Lights with your smartphone & tablet apps**	**o**
2.1	If you have an opportunity to install wires (i.e. renovation or new build) then install a wired based whole-house lighting control system	o
2.2	Otherwise, if you are like many of us and your home is not pre-wired for lighting control, go ahead and install some HA 2.0 smart plugs and light switches.	o
3.0	**Use your HA 2.0 system to save money on your electricity bills.**	**o**
3.1	Install HA 2.0 modules that reduce electricity wasted by your lights & kitchen appliances.	o
3.2	Install smart thermostats to automate your in-home heating and cooling systems.	o
3.3	Interface a home energy monitoring unit with your HA 2.0 controller	o
4.0	**Integrate an MRM 2.0 sytem into your home**	**o**
4.1	Plan your requirements	o
4.2	Install either a wired or a wireless MRM 2.0 system	o
4.3	Try to also get some music going out the back garden!	o

5.0	Setup a system that distributes the HD content coming out of your various TV sources to other rooms around the house.	o
5.1	Plan your HDTV system and establish a budget	o
5.2	Install either a Cat6, Powerline or Wireless HDTV distribution system	o
6.0	Add a Home Cinema to your HA 2.0 System	o
6.1	Try to assign an area in your house and build out a proper 5.1 home cinema system.	o
6.2	Setup a Wi-Fi to IR system that allows you to control everything from your smart phone or tablet!	o

Please remember that HA 2.0 does allow for a certain flexibility of picking and choosing. So feel free to pick out the features that appeal the most and forget about the rest.

Thanks!